GOD,
ARE YOU *for* REAL?

GOD, ARE YOU *for* REAL?

David Bateman

XULON PRESS

Xulon Press
2301 Lucien Way #415
Maitland, FL 32751
407.339.4217
www.xulonpress.com

© 2019 by David Bateman

All rights reserved solely by the author. The author guarantees all contents are original and do not infringe upon the legal rights of any other person or work. No part of this book may be reproduced in any form without the permission of the author. The views expressed in this book are not necessarily those of the publisher.

Unless otherwise indicated, Scripture quotations taken from the New American Standard Bible (NASB). Copyright © 1960, 1962, 1963, 1968, 1971, 1972, 1973, 1975, 1977, 1995 by The Lockman Foundation. Used by permission. All rights reserved.

Printed in the United States of America.

ISBN-13: 978-1-5456-7891-6

TABLE OF CONTENTS

FOREWORD ix

CHAPTER I: Demographics by Generation 1

CHAPTER II: Religiosity by Generation–Many Different Religions and Worldviews. 11

CHAPTER III: Impact of Culture/Sociology On Religious Worldview 45

CHAPTER IV: Impact of Relativism/Humanism/Secularism/Materialism/Scientism On The Religious Worldview 49

CHAPTER V: Recent Polls and Surveys On Reasons For Youth Leaving The Christian Faith. 55

CHAPTER VI: Christian Responses to Reasons for Leaving The Christain Faith 75

CHAPTER VII: Spiritual Indifference, "Nones" and Evangelizing The "Whatever" Generation. 185

CHAPTER VIII : The Challenge of Making The Right Decision . 201

ABOUT THE AUTHOR. 205

FOREWORD

We definitely live in interesting times. Science and technology continually uncover new medicines and health opportunities to give us greater quality of life and to extend longevity. I am convinced it won't be long until we can reasonably expect to live 120+ years. After all, it is recorded in Old Testament scripture that many, like Abraham, commonly lived that long.

We have conquered near space and the moon. Americans are talking about more trips to the moon and eventually to Mars, most probably within our lifetimes. The economy is booming, creating many new jobs and entrepreneurial opportunities. Copious funds and technology are available to move us into a new era of invention and technical tools. New technologies seem to double computing capacity every two years (Moore's Law). Humankind has made astonishing advances in quality of life through technology, educational and business opportunities, communication capabilities, and computing capacity. And AI is just around the corner. Social media allows instantaneous communication with anyone anywhere in the world. Search engines such as Google bring every new writing, thought, concept, and communication into our homes. Virtually every document ever created in the history of humankind is now available at the fingertips. One can now research any topic within milliseconds.

Facebook allows instant communication of trending ideas among followers worldwide. LinkedIn is a good platform for business networking. Video sharing includes YouTube, which provides video media outlets for any idea conceivable. Micro-blogging includes companies like Twitter, which allows short instantaneous 140-character bursts with anyone around the world. Apple provides state-of-the-art communication devices. Amazon allows us to purchase virtually any product in the world with a keystroke. These are now trillion-dollar companies because they have successfully captured their respective markets, and investors are shoveling more funds toward them to grow these companies even more. Each of these companies has a greater net worth than many of the world's nations. There is also greater division of wealth between haves and have-nots. More of our younger generations can find jobs than ever before; however, many cannot afford to buy their own homes and choose to live with their parents instead, well into their thirties and forties. Many are holding off on marriage and having children later in their lives when finances stabilize.

Technology, and science are advancing at warp speed. An example is the iPhone. Nearly everyone has one. They are unquestionably wonderful devices, allowing instantaneous communication—as fast as one can conceive a thought, it is literally being received at the other end of the wireless network. Same with emails—virtually no time lag. What a leap from 100 years ago when we were still sending letters by snail mail or possibly a wire by telegraph or landline telephone. Amazing advancements. However, they are not without casualties.

Today's youth is more inclined to email, text, or phone a friend. In-person meetings are becoming passé. Business is being conducted from home more and more, with fewer in-person meetings. There definitely are efficiencies built into our new technology, but there are also severe drawbacks—less interpersonal communication and contact. The net result is less personal expression of eye contact, personalized emotion between people resulting in a centralization of the inter-social contacts being limited to oneself. Because so much is available on the Internet, one does not have to interact as much with others to get answers to questions. Just dial up Google, or email the experts. Again, the pros and cons, yin and yang, good and bad. These factors are definitely affecting the youth of today, and not always for the better. We shall explore how these advances lead to certain harmful philosophies that need to be exposed, understood, and dealt with: humanism, secularism, relativism, scientism, and materialism. Many youth today are raising the question whether there is there a God, and if so, where is God in this mix?

All of these technological advances around the world have brought humankind to new, previously unreachable frontiers—science and technology, education, health, business, and extended life are all good. But who can legitimately claim credit for these advances? Where does this spirit of innovation and advancement emanate from? Our individual minds? Spirits? Are we truly masters of our own lives and destinies? Or are we influenced by subconscious insights and intuition starting in our spirits and moving into our minds for implementation? Why does society and the well-being of humankind seem to generally continue to advance in a positive and ever improving and increasingly interesting and technologically enticing manner, as opposed to a backward direction with death and destruction, as exemplified with conflicts, warfare or terrorism? Are we being protected by supernatural forces? Are we being threatened? What forces are behind these opposed positions? Are we in a battle of principalities at the spiritual level? Or are all of these yin and yang, good and evil, positive and negative vibes merely fictions generated in the human mind or heart and spirit? Are they for real or imagined? Are we truly the masters and captains of our own ships (lives)? Are there supernatural beings, both good and evil, fighting over our very spirits/souls? If the supernatural, which is unseen by any of us mere mortals, truly exists, are those forces for us or against us? Where is God in this fray? These are some of the underlying questions and themes discussed in this book.

Where are society and human relationships trending? Is there a secular or spiritual moral compass? How do our youth distinguish between right and wrong? Where is the line in the sand? Daily news is inundated with vicious politics, vitriolic name-calling, mudslinging and general calumny. Where is line between spirited debate and mean-spirited attack? What happened to the days of respectful debate and discussion?

During my many years as a lawyer and litigator, I saw the sad digression of spirited arguments in the courtroom focused on the case and legal issues at hand to degrading personal ad hominem attacks between counsel. Lawyers bent on winning their respective cases no matter the cost or collateral damage between the advocates. The judge would often have to step in to bring decorum back to the proceedings. What is the thinking behind these personal attacks, which in my mind do nothing but digress from seeking out the truth for the legal issue at hand? Attempts at unsettling the opposing counsel and parties? Where is the mutual respect and dignity demonstrated in this legal setting? I fully understand the heat of the courtroom battle, but what happened to basic decency and civility in trying a case? Most judges won't tolerate this conduct and will often reprimand offending counsel. In my experience these diversionary tactics do not enhance that attorney's legal position. To the contrary most judges do not find them helpful in seeking out the truth. And these personal attacks are certainly not blessed by a Christian God. Other forces are obviously at work. I bring up this example to make the point that I believe there are supernatural principalities and forces, both good and bad, constantly at work on each spirit and soul. We are definitely not alone in this physical world. There are supernatural forces at work

Each individual may have a different subjective concept of right and wrong (morality) and spirituality. This is called relativism.

FOREWORD

Herein lies part of the conflict. Some individuals are spiritually grounded, while others are unaffiliated and unconnected to any higher spiritual authority. This is called secularism, materialism, and humanism. Herein lies the other part of the conflict. These are the new realities cropping up in our societies. We need to recognize these differences and deal with them. That is an underlying theme of this book.

I have seen similar examples in both simple and complex business dealings. Truth and honesty in business seems to be waning. Each side tries to gain the upper hand in a deal. That's fine. That is what business is about. But what is not fine is unscrupulous misrepresentations, lies, and false promises to set the deal up only to pull the plug on the deal later on the unsuspecting party. They then drop the hammer when the time is right to gain an unfair financial advantage. My legal experience is that the courtroom is often used as an extended boardroom. Drive the deal to a trial, making spurious and frivolous claims, racking up large attorney's fees, and basically outspending and maneuvering the opponent to gain an unfair advantage and to extract additional consideration in the deal. Thankfully, arbitration, or mediation, reduces the exorbitant expenses of a full trial. Each of the party litigants are forced to go through a risk-benefit analysis to see what additional benefits might come from litigating a point that was not adequately covered in the original agreement or that the other side is frivolously pursuing. Good news for lawyers—there will always be gainful employment. Some say this is just business. OK, I get it, but I suggest we start turning the rhetoric and one-upmanship heat down a bit. Let's try to work out actual or potential legal issues civilly and in good faith. Both sides need to take a more conciliatory approach to resolving business disputes. Negotiate the deal well, taking hard and strong positions, but do so honestly and with integrity in the process. I suggest the parties not try to take unfair advantage of the other. And when it comes to dispute resolution, be more conciliatory and understanding of the other side's position. Don't cave or allow the other side to walk over you like a doormat, but be open to early resolution of the dispute. Perhaps some old-fashioned neighborly love, called for in the Bible, might be appropriate. I say this is doing business by the Book! Do it God's way. Follow the moral compass. Guaranteed it will save the parties both financial and emotional pain and stress.

The same concepts above apply to our everyday lives in marriage, families, friendships, office settings, and in the classroom. Each of these relationships has its challenges. Sometimes we experience hard times with the relationship closed off. Each side of the dispute takes a strong and hardened stand, digging one's heels in. Again, can we bring the moral compass and guidelines into the fray to resolve the conflict? Do we even think about how God views the relational dispute and how He would like to see it resolved? I firmly believe that as long as there are two people on earth, there will be conflict. The challenge is to figure out how to resolve the conflict so everyone can experience an inner peace. Can we find that moral compass and inner voice to help? I believe we can! We'll explore the concept of the moral compass in some detail in this book.

Life is full of twists and turns. The human condition is truly a multifaceted, multidimensional, and complicated one. It is true that human beings are very complex creatures working at the physical, mental, and spiritual levels. These levels interact constantly to allow each of us to function for good or for evil. We know this as a matter of proven fact, which we shall explore in this book. One of the underlying themes of this book is to search out and explore the truth of the many metaphysical philosophies, spirituality, and the major religious worldviews. We'll then apply them to our younger generations based on extensive survey research to see where our youth are spiritually and then address the alarming trend of mass exodus from their Christian heritage as they move forward in this life. The gut question is whether there is any longer a place for spirituality in their lives. Or are the forces of humanism, secularism, materialism, scientism, and relativism winning over their souls? Is Satan distracting our youth into a sense of self-centricity and dependency and away from Christocentric living and dependence on God in this life? Good and evil supernatural forces are at work to capture souls. To identify these forces and deal with them is part of critical thinking and a major theme in this book.

The supernatural exists, and therein, I believe we can find the answers to the questions about the essence, meaning, and purpose of life. It is not just some theoretical spiritual or religious concept that makes for good debate. It is real. I believe that God is real and that our spiritual side strongly impacts the mental and physical sides in each of our lives.

Whether you are spiritual, a monotheist, a polytheist, or an agnostic or atheist, I know you will find this book engaging in testing your spiritual beliefs and worldviews. I hope to challenge your thinking about your spiritual beliefs and aspirations. I hope to prove you in the end that the Christian God is real, that He loves you beyond anything imaginable, and that His will is truly to prosper you and not to harm you. I shall share with you the argument that all you need to do in response to His freely given grace is to believe in His Son Jesus Christ, repent of your sins, and move forward in life doing good and loving God and your fellow men and women. Where is God? Is God for real? How do we find Him? We shall challenge, discuss, argue, and discover the answer to these questions throughout this book.

As for the spiritual impact on our youth, we know from recent polls and articles that our younger generations are trending away from Christian beliefs, regular church attendance, and spiritual inclinations in their lives. As many as 40% Christians of all ages and at least 50% of millennials have left the Christian church! In recent Pew surveys, they mark themselves down as "nones," with no religious affiliation. Many authors, including myself, relate this movement over the last 30 years to millennials (Y Gen) and the Z Generation moving away from spirituality toward new readily accessible alternative scientific explanations for the wonders of our universe, individualistic assessments as to the purpose of life, and unique individual beliefs on a life after death. We also see youth adopting the self-sufficient philosophy of relativism to address their individual concepts of right and wrong, i.e., their own moral compass. Secularism, materialism, and humanism are now beginning to supplant objective spiritual beliefs about a supernatural God.

In other words, I see a movement among the younger generations away from traditional truths about our existence and the existence of God and a devotion to God the Father (Creator), the Son (Savior), and the Holy Spirit (presence of Jesus with us and the Messenger to the end of time)—three individual but consubstantial known as The Trinity. Any religious affiliation seems to be waning in favor of subjective beliefs on spirits, religions, worldviews, philosophies, and "gods" that fit one's individual agendas. We see personal beliefs of our younger generations becoming more self-centered and less God centered.

According to the poll research, young people are leaving the Christian church for many reasons including: "Not relevant to my life"; " Science trumps religion"; "Christianity is not working for me"; "Christianity and religion do not make logical or reasoned sense to me"; "I don't believe in God or Jesus"; "No one ever explained the faith to me"; "The Internet has all the the answers I need to understand life"; "Christian beliefs are not based on solid evidence of fact–all hearsay with no credible documents to prove authenticity"; "I find my god elsewhere"; " I get nothing out of a Christian service; it means nothing to me"; "Science refutes Christianity"; and "Christians are hypocrites." Do you relate to any

FOREWORD

of these arguments against God and the Christian faith? If you do, this book is for you!

This is a very dangerous trend, in my opinion. I am convinced that none of us will ever realize the serious consequences of this trend in our lives today and into the life hereafter. I believe that we cannot experience a truly complete and fulfilled life here on earth and certainly never realize eternal happiness, joy, and peace with God in the life hereafter if we remain on this dangerous course. One of the purposes of this book is to highlight the proven spiritual truths and paint clear distinctions for you to consider in choosing a future path through this life—with or without God. To this end, we shall explore these trends, applying scientific data and scriptural and historical truths about God, and address each of the likely reasons for this trend with solid Christian evidence and responses. However, in the end you will have to make an individual judgment as to what you believe and what direction you will pursue.

CHAPTER I

Demographics by Generation

Demographics. I thought it useful to break down our cohorts into logical demographic groupings, based on the social, economic, and spiritual dynamics, to see how large a part religion or spirituality plays within each of those group dynamics. I used traditional birth date demographics as our background for analysis–baby boomers (1946–64), Gen X (1965–80), Gen Y (1981–95) (millennials), and Gen Z (1996–present). They demonstrate enough demarcation and uniqueness that I felt there was enough scientific and sociological legitimacy to break down the sense of the bigger questions in life.

In contrast, however, Matthew Hennessy, at *CityJournal.org*, comments and cautions us on using the generation divide as an analytic base:

> *"Many balk at using the concept of generations as a lens through which to analyze political, cultural, social, and economic trends, as if tens of millions of people could possibly be of one mind—or even similar minds—about important matters. University of California at Berkeley political scientist Laura Stoker calls the notion that you can divide the populace into discrete generations "fruitful if vexing." It may be silly to assume that Americans born in 1965 would have precisely—or even nearly—the same attitudes and*

opinions as those born in 1980. But they are likely to share at least a common vocabulary, as Stoker notes, "by virtue of having experienced a specific set of social, economic, technological, and/or political circumstances at a formative period in their lives." Viewing the world through the lens of generations is no more or less legitimate than viewing it through the lenses of gender, race, class, or immigration status. These broad frames are the conceptual tools available to us, and it's not clear what better alternatives exist. "Generational boundaries are fuzzy, arbitrary and culture-driven," acknowledge Pew researchers Paul Taylor and George Gao in a 2014 study of Generation X, but "once fixed by the mysterious forces of the zeitgeist, they tend to firm up over time."[1]

However, I feel that there is enough validity and group commonality in the generational divide demarcation, to comfortably use it as a valid tool for our limited analysis of people groups in America as to their spirituality. I have, therefore, created the following demographic matrix for each group:

---

[1] Hennessy, Matthew, Zero Hour for Generation X, Cityjournal.org.

Generation   Birth Dates
Baby Boomers[2]   1946–1964

Characteristics

76 million[3]; Income and standard of living improved worldwide; greater longevity economy; $7 trillion in goods and services annually; 75% use the Internet and 25% use social media; longer retirements but less savings (40% have $0); many took hits in the Great Recession—high mortgages and debt; era of free sex and drugs. US Religions—78% are Christian, 2% Jewish, 1% Muslim, 1% Buddhist, unaffiliated "nones," 17%, atheist 2%, agnostic 2%.[4] 59% say religion is very important.[5] 92% believe in a God and 65% in the God of the Bible.[6]

---

[2] Investopedia, Generation X, 1.

[3] Wikipedia, Baby Boomers, at Section 2.1, Size and Impact

[4] Pew Research Center, *Religion and Public Life, Religious Landscape Study, Baby Boomers* (2017).

[5] Pew Research Center, *By Many Measures Millennials Are Less Religious*, (November 20, 2015); Stroebel, Lee, *The Case for Christ,: A Journalist's Personal Investigation of the Evidence for Christ* (Zondervan, Harper and Collins Publishers (2017), 163 – in 2014 Stroebel conducted a national poll of 1,001 individuals, through the Barna Group, and found that 82% of Boomers are certain God exists, while only 62% of Millennials believe that God exists.

[6] Pew Research Center, *When Americans Say they Believe in God, What do They Mean?* (April 25, 2018)

Generation   Birth Dates
X Generation[7]   1965–1980

Characteristics
65 Million[8]; Dot Com bust; 2008 financial crisis; Great recession; more self-directed than boomers; tech savvy and online; use financial advisors more than boomers; invest heavily in ETFs; 68% of CEOs in Fortune 500 companies; $11 trillion in wealth in 2015, and boomers will transfer over $37 trillion to Gen X by 2037; more conservative than millennials but less partisan than boomers; grew up in era of prosperity, social stability and racial equality; active, balanced, and happy life–only 4% were unhappy; era of continuing experimentation with free sex, drugs; divorce rate peaked in 1980s; difficulty saving for retirement like boomers; delay deciding on retirement, and may work longer; US Religions–70% declare they are Christian; 67% say religion very important; 76% believe in God.[9]

---

[7] Investopedia, Baby Boomer, 1; Hennessy, supra.

[8] Chase, Jessica, *The Religious Beliefs of Baby Boomers, Generation X, and the Millennials: There Still are Gender Differences*, (MA University of Central Florida, 2013), 12.

[9] Pew Research Center, *Adults in Generation X Who Are Christian* (2014); Pew Research Center, *Religious Landscape Study* (2014).

Generation   Birth Dates
Y Generation/Millennials[10]   1981–1995

Characteristics

Obama Era; make up over half of the work force; impatient with traditional business practices; want to move up faster in the ranks; they move between jobs at a much higher rate than their predecessors; have been called 83 Million[11]; "lazy, entitled narcissists"[12] They have high self-esteem.[13] Less political than boomers or Gen Xers–nothing special about being an American–more inclined to socialism;[14] inclined toward restricting offensive speech–at the expense of free speech; technology and the Internet define millennials; they favor moving human interaction to the Internet; they appreciate the "sharing economy" of the Internet; the majority prefers texting rather than talking; effects on the brain has increased ADD/HD 43% from 2003 to 2011[15]; bridge between analog boomers (cultivated patience) and digital (cultivated impatience);[16] individualistic, millennials independent, resourceful and self-sufficient; two-income families; value freedom and responsibilities; technologically adept (scientism)–moving from manufacturing to a service economy; adapt well to change and are

---

[10] Wikipedia, Millennials.

[11] Id, at Section 6, Demographics; Bureau, US Census. "*Millennials Outnumber Baby Boomers and Are Far More Diverse*". www.census.gov. Retrieved 5 October 2015; Wikipedia, *Millennials, Section 6, Demographics*.

[12] Hennessy, supra, referring to a 2013 *Time Magazine* cover story article by Joel Stein.

[13] Hennessy, supra.

[14] Id.

[15] Id.

[16] Id.

tolerant to alternative lifestyles; they work to live rather than live to work—work-life balance;[17] work centric, independent, goal oriented, competitive, self-actualizing;[18] special, sheltered, confident, team-oriented, conventional, pressured, and achieving.[19] Less than half of the men and women want children.[20] Politics–supportive of a progressive domestic agenda[21] US Religion–4% claim to be atheists and 3% agnostics–40% are "nones" and 38% are religious.[22] 52% believe in a Biblical God and 41% say religion is important.[23]– by contrast over 50% of millennials in England had no religion or attended a place of worship.[24]

---

[17] Wikipedia, Millennials, Section 3, Traits

[18] Kane, Sally, *The Common Characteristics of Generation X Professionals*, (thebalancecareers.com, updated April 19, 2018)

[19] Wikipedia, Millennials, Section 3, Traits

[20] Id, at Section 8, Peter Pan Generation.

[21] Id, at Section 11, Cultural Identity

[22] Id, at Section 9, Religion; "Religion Among the Millennials", Pew Research Center. (www.pewresearch.org, February 17, 2010); Lipka, Michael, *Millennials Increasingly are Driving Growth of "Nones,"* FactTank News in the Numbers (www.pewresearch.org, May 12, 2015).

[23] Pew Research, *"Religion among Millennials"* supra; Pew Research Center, When Americans Say they Believe in God, What do They Mean? (April 25, 2018); By Many Measures, Millennials are Less Religious, Pew Research Center (www.pewresearch.com, November 20, 2015).

[24] Wikipedia, supra

Generation   Birth Dates
Generation Z[25] 1996–present

Characteristics
82 million[26]; characteristics—cynical, private, (Post Millennial) entrepreneurial, multi-tasking, hyperaware, technology reliant,[27] technology cultural diversity, pragmatism.[28] Other characteristics are: Internet experts, rather message than talk in person, look up to U-Tubers; 9/11 was large part of youth; recession affected outlooks, determined to turn hobbies into jobs, they are one step ahead in their careers, they are self-starters, they are often stressed out, they prioritize quality, they are more accepting,[29] US Religion—Belief in God of the Bible—39% "nones."[30] 41% church attendance compared to 18% for Millennials at the same ages, 21% for Generation X, and 26% for baby boomers. This church attendance figure may be misleading as churches may adjust their messages to fit the audience.

---

[25] WIlliams, Alex, *Move Over Millennials, Here Comes Generation Z* (New York Times, September 3, 2015; Wikipedia, Generation Z, at Section 1, Terminology

[26] American Fact Finder, US Census Bureau, 2016 Census (Ages 5–19),

[27] Elmore, Tim, *Growing Leaders, 6 Defining Characteristics of Generation Z*, (www.growingleaders.com, September 15, 2015).

[28] Ryan, Scott, Get Ready for Generation Z, Cause Cast (Forbes/Leadership, November 28, 2016)

[29] Paige, Ashley, Popsugar US (Yahoo Lifestyle, April 22, 2017)

[30] Merritt, Jonathan, *Forget Millennials, How Will Church Reach Generation Z?*, Religion News Service (May 1, 2017); Pew Research Center, *When Americans Say they Believe in God, What do They Mean?* (April 25, 2018)

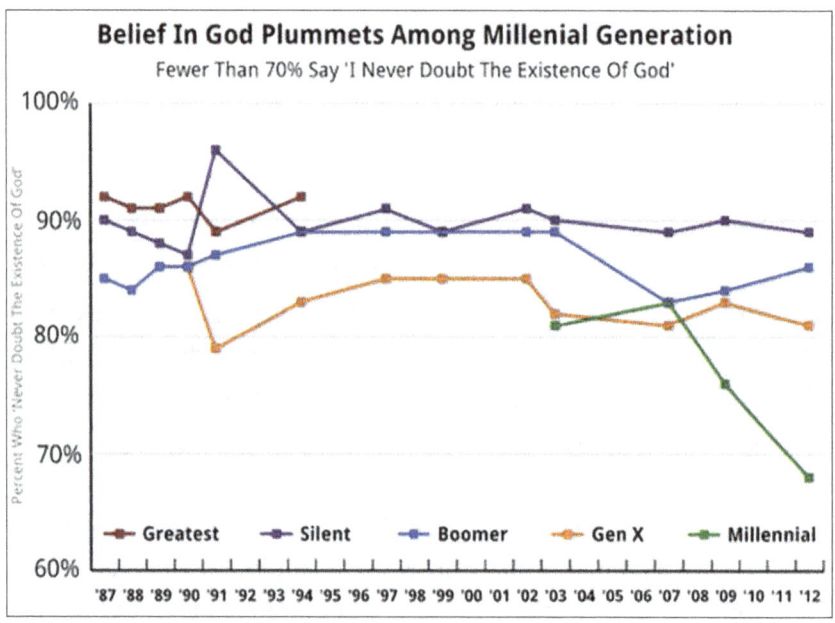

31

I attribute some of the sharp reduction in profession of a faith, at least partially, to lack of spiritual structure at home and not learning from others about faith, peer pressure, feeling unwelcome, and a movement socially more to the left (socialism) than to the right (conservatism).[32] Additional factors include a sense of financial and social well-being, and finally, partially to the effects of scientism, humanism, secularism, materialism, and relativism (the five "ism's"). There is, today, less dependence on God or other supernatural spiritual being to get along in life, among our youth, than ever before. This dissociation is both compelling and alarming.

For example, some pundits declare that science and faith are incompatible; therefore, the Hobson's choice of one or the other.

---

[31] Spitzer, Fr Robert, *Essential 2: Proof of God's Existence from Science* (Credible Catholic, www.crediblecatholic.com, 2017), slide 4; Pew Research Center.

[32] Hertzenberg, Stephanie, *Why Millennials are Really Leaving Religion: It's Not Just Politics*, Beliefnet (www.beliefnet.com)

Fortunately, most millennials still have a place for some form of faith in their hearts and spirits and for science and reason in their minds.[33] Contrary to naysayer claims, I contend these two concepts can coexist within a person. They are not incompatible or mutually exclusive.

---

[33] Spitzer, supra, slide 9.

CHAPTER II

Religiosity by Generation– Many Different Religions and Worldviews

There are many different religions, belief systems, and traditions prevalent in the world:

1. **Monotheistic Religions**[34]–God centered; eternal consequences of evil–evil is defined differently; relationships between God, you, and your neighbor differ.[35]
a. **Catholic Christianity**–largest Christian church with over 1.3 billion members worldwide. It is a Trinitarian faith, founded by Jesus Christ, 2,000 years ago. St Peter was the first Pope.[36] The church is directed by revelations of the Holy Spirit, through Scripture and traditions of the church.[37] The Magisterium

---

[34] Wikipedia, Monotheism, 1–11.

[35] David Bateman, *You, Me and God: Intimate Relationships: (A Missionary Handbook)*, (Xulon Press, Salem Publishing, 2018), 16-20

[36] Wikipedia, Catholic Church, 1.

[37] Id, at Section 3, Doctrine; *"CCC, 80–81".* Vatican.va. Archived from the original on June 29, 2011. Retrieved June 30, 2011; *Paul VI, Pope (1964).* "Lumen Gentium, chapter 2, Paragraph 14". Vatican. Archived from the original on September 6, 2014. Retrieved March 9, 2008.

starting with the Pope and the College of Bishops interpret Scripture and Tradition.[38] These are authoritatively stated and explained in the Catechism of the Catholic Church.[39] Catholics are Trinitarian and believe in the Holy Trinity—God the Father, God the Son, and God the Holy Spirit.[40] Jesus Christ, the only begotten Son of God, came to earth as both human and divine to reconcile and reunite mankind with God the Father, after the fall of Adam and Eve through original sin.[41] Because of original sin we all experience death. And, we were all spiritually lost. Jesus reconciled that condition through His death and resurrection. He reestablished our relationship with the Father, as long as we repent of our sins and believe in Jesus. This is called justification. According to the dogma of the Catholic Church, the Holy Spirit was then sent by God the Father and God the Son to carry on the work of Jesus in the new reestablished relationship between Heaven and earth after Jesus' death and resurrection.[42]

---

[38] Id; "The Teaching Office". Catechism of the Catholic Church. Vatican. Archived from the original on 6 September 2010. Retrieved 24 July 2010; "CCC, 85–88". Vatican.va. Archived from the original on 29 June 2011. Retrieved 30 June, 2011.

[39] Id; *John Paul II, Pope "Laetamur Magnopere".* (Vatican, 1997). Archived from the original on March 14, 2015. Retrieved March 21, 2015.

[40] Id, at Section 3.1, Nature of God; "CCC, 232–237; 252". Vatican.va. Retrieved 21 March 2015" CCC, 232–237; 252". Vatican.va. Retrieved March 21, 2015.

[41] Id; *"CCC, 'Jesus Christ suffered under Pontius Pilate, was crucified, died, and was buried'".* Vatican.va. Retrieved December 30, 2014; "CCC, 608". Vatican.va. Retrieved August 6, 2014.

[42] Id; *"Greek and Latin Traditions on Holy Spirit".* ewtn.com; *"CCC, 'Jesus Christ suffered under Pontius Pilate, was crucified, died, and was buried'".* Vatican.va. Retrieved December 30, 2014.

Each person has a spiritual soul which will transcend physical death of the body/mind and will be initially judged by Jesus Christ; Jesus and God the Father will be present at the second judgment.[43] Each soul will spend eternity in the presence of God, in Heaven, or outside His presence, in Hell.[44] Catholics believe that mankind can realize Heaven through this reconciliation brought through the life, death, and resurrection of Jesus Christ.[45] Salvation and eternal life with God, according to the Catholic tradition, comes through 1) believing in Jesus Christ as the saving and atoning Son of God the Fathertrue repentance and sorrow for one's sins and baptism by water (justification), and 2) repentance and confession of sins after baptism, and leading a life of love for God and neighbor as exemplified by good deeds (sanctification).[46]

The church is the continuing presence of Jesus Christ and the Holy Spirit on earth.[47] Catholics worship only God, but honor and venerate saints of the church who led exemplary lives and are examples of how one should lead one's life.[48] Peter was the rock upon which the church was built. He is the first Bishop (Pope)

---

[43] Id, at Section 3.3, Final Judgment; "CCC, 1021–22, 1039, 1051". *Vatican.va. Retrieved 28 December, 2014. CCC 1039: ...The Last Judgment will reveal even to its furthest consequences the good each person has done or failed to do during his earthly life"*

[44] Id, *"CCC, 1023–29, 1042–50". Vatican.va. Retrieved 30 July 2014.;* "CCC, 1033–37, 1057". Vatican.va, Retrieved August 7, 2014.

[45] Id; "CCC, 608". Vatican.va. Retrieved August 6, 2014.

[46] John 3:14–21; Mark 1:15; James 2:14–26.

[47] Id, at Section 3.2, Nature of the Church.

[48] Id, at Section 3.4, Virgin Mary and Devotions; *"Pope Benedict XVI- Feast of Solemnity of the Blessed Virgin Mary".* Vatican.va. 1 January 2012. Archived from the original on July 2, 2012. Retrieved 17 August, 2012; Wikipedia, List of Saints.

of Rome.[49] The Bible does not restrict faith to the written word only. The first Christians did not have the first writings of the New Testament (Sacred Scripture) until about AD 130. And it was not until AD 397 that the Bible, consisting of 73 books, was officially assembled. Most of the New Testament was written beginning many years after the death of Jesus. The Church was, early on, built on the inspired traditional beliefs (sacred tradition) of its followers, i.e., the tradition of the Catholic Church.[50]

The center of Catholic orthodoxy is the celebration of the Eucharistic liturgy (Thanksgiving) at Mass–thanksgiving for the death and resurrection of Jesus Christ, who opened the door to Heaven again, so that we have the opportunity to share eternity with God, the saints, and relatives, friends and strangers who believed in Jesus and led good lives.[51] The Eucharist is the central part of the Mass, where the bread and wine are transubstantiated into the actual body and blood of Jesus in commemoration

---

[49] Matthew 16:18; Wikipedia, St Peter, 1.

[50] Horn, Trent, *Why We're Catholic: Our Reasons for Faith, Hope, and Love* (Catholic Answers Press, 2017), 76.

[51] Wikipedia, Eucharist in the Catholic Church.

of His saving grace for his followers.[52] St Paul tells followers of Jesus to stand firm and hold to the traditions of which one was taught by word of mouth or by letter (2 Thess. 2:15). Catholics and Protestants jointly believe in the Sacred Scripture, which is the canon of Scripture, which was declared at the Council of Hippo in AD 393 and Carthage in AD 397, establishing the 73 books of the Catholic Bible but only 66 books in the Protestant Bible with the sixteenth-century Lutheran-led Protestant movement. The Protestant movement deleted the deuterocanonicals from the Old Testament (not part of the original part of the Hebrew bible, Pentateuch or Torah). Those books are: Sirach, Tobit, 1 and 2 Maccabees, Judith, Wisdom, Baruch and additions to Esther and Daniel. [53] The foundation to the Catholic faith is based on sacred Scripture, which includes the Bible (written tradition) as interpreted

---

[52] Id, at Section 4, Sacraments of Christian Initiation, Eucharist; *Pohle, Joseph "The Real Presence of Christ in the Eucharist"* In Herbermann, Charles. Catholic Encyclopedia. (New York: Robert Appleton Company, 1913).; "CCC, 1392–95". Vatican.va. Retrieved 23 November 2014; Id, New Testament Foundations at Section 1.1—"The Catholic Church sees as the main basis for this belief the words of Jesus himself at his Last Supper: the Synoptic Gospels (Matthew 26-28; Mark 14:22-24; Luke 22:19-20) and Saint Paul's 1 Corinthians 11:23–25 recount that in that context Jesus said of what to all appearances were bread and wine: "This is my body ... this is my blood." The Gospel of John in Chapter 6, *The Discourse on the Bread of Life*, presents Jesus as saying: "Unless you eat the flesh of the Son of Man and drink his blood, you do not have life within you... Whoever eats my flesh and drinks my blood remains in me and I in him" (John 6:53-56). "" Saint Paul implied an identity between the apparent bread and wine of the Eucharist and the body and blood of Christ, when he wrote: "The cup of blessing that we bless, is it not a participation in the blood of Christ? The bread that we break, is it not a participation in the body of Christ? (1 Corinthians 10:16)" and elsewhere: "Therefore whoever eats the bread or drinks the cup of the Lord unworthily will have to answer for the body and blood of the Lord" (1 Corinthians 11:27)"; Wikipedia, Id, Section 3.1, Transubstantiation.

[53] Horn, Trent, supra at 78-79; Horn, Trent, *The Old Testament Canon, the Case for Catholicism, Answers to Classic and Contemporary Protestant Objections* (Ignatius Press, San Francisco, 2017), 35, 49, 54.

through the sacred tradition, including both written and oral tradition to interpret Sacred Scripture.[54] This Tradition can be found in the Catechism of the Catholic Church.

   b. **Protestant Christianity**—Protestantism is the second largest segment within Christianity, with collectively more than 900 million adherents worldwide or nearly 40% of all Christians.[55] It is a Trinitarian faith, believing in the Father, Son, and Holy Spirit–three distinct persons constituting a single God. Protestantism originated with Martin Luther in 1517, with the Reformation/Revolution,[56] when he nailed his 95 theses on the Wittenberg church door protesting, among other things, the Catholic Church selling of indulgences.[57] Ever since, Protestants have railed against the Catholic Church teachings on the sacraments and papal supremacy.[58] They called the Pope the Antichrist. They disagree on the theology of the real presence in the bread and wine.[59] "The more progressive churches emphasize the priesthood of all believers, justification by faith alone (*sola fide*) rather than by good works, and the highest authority of the Bible alone (do not believe in Catholic sacred

---

[54] Horn, *Why we are Catholic*, supra, at 80.

[55] Wikipedia, Protestantism; "Pewforum: Christianity (2010)" (PDF). Retrieved 14 May 2014; "Christianity 2015: Religious Diversity and Personal Contact" (PDF). gordonconwell.edu. January 2015. Retrieved 29 May 2015; "CCC–Global Statistics". Retrieved 5 December 2015.

[56] Wikipedia, supra; Protestants: A History from Wittenberg to Pennsylvania 1517–1740, 15.

[57] Id.

[58] Id; Protestants: A History from Wittenberg to Pennsylvania 1517–1740, 32 and 50.

[59] Id.

tradition) in faith and morals (*sola scriptura*)."[60] "The "Five Solae" summarize basic theological differences in opposition to the Roman Catholic Church."[61] They are: 1) sola scriptura (by scripture alone) (scripture over tradition of the church), 2) sola fide (by faith alone) (faith over works) (justification), 3) sola gratia (by grace alone) (not by merit), 4) solus Christus (salvation and forgiveness of sins through Christ alone) (no mediators or intermediaries–priests–are necessary), and 5) soli deo gloria (glory to God alone) (Mary and saints not to be worshipped or glorified).[62] There are a multitude of denominations within the Protestant faith–Adventists (e.g., Seventh Day Adventists), Anglicans, Baptists, Reformed (Calvinism), Lutherans, Methodists, and Pentecostals/Evangelicals e.g., Assemblies of God. Nondenominational, and charismatic churches, not affiliated with mainstream Protestant denominations, are on the rise.[63] "Protestants reject the Roman Catholic Church's doctrine that it is the one true church believing in the *invisible church*, which consists of all who profess faith in Jesus Christ."[64] Protestants do not believe in the traditions of the Catholic church. Currently there are over 40,000 independent denominations of Protestants worldwide. There are at least 200 major Protestant denominations or denominational groupings in the United States. A number of protestant

---

[60] Id; Mothering the Fatherland: A Protestant Sisterhood Repents for the Holocaust by George Faithful, p.159.

[61] Id; Philip Voerding: The Trouble with Christianity: A Concise Outline of Christian History.

[62] Wikipedia, Five Solae, 1

[63] Wikipedia, Protestantism, 1; *"Pewforum: Christianity (2010)" (PDF). Retrieved May 14, 2014*

[64] Id, at Section 5.1, Denominations;Fr. John Morris: An Orthodox Response to the Recent Roman Catholic Declaration on the Nature of the Church.

denominations are working toward reunification with the Catholic Church. Ironically, Lutherans lead this effort.[65]

c. **Orthodox Christianity**—Refers to doctrines believed by early Christians.[66] Both Orthodox and Christian beliefs are based on the First Seven Ecumenical Councils held over seven centuries. 1) The First Council of Nicaea (325 AD) sided with Homousianism holding to true Trinitarian beliefs and held non-Trinitarian Arianism, that Jesus Christ was not equal to God the Father, to be heresy. The Council determined that Jesus Christ was the Son of God the Father and existed for all time with Him. He was consubstantial (same substance) with the Father as stated in the Nicene Creed of 325, which was also adopted and is still recited by mainstream Christians.[67] 2) The First Council of Constantinople (381) modified the work of the earlier Council of Nicaea, repudiated Arianism, and revised the Nicene Creed to add the Holy Spirit as the third person of the Holy Trinity.[68] 3) The First Council of Ephesus (431) repudiated Nestorianism, and declared Mary to be Theotokos and

---

[65] The National Catholic Register, Blogs, Status of Global Christianity, 2017, in the Context of 1900–2050, Center for Global Christianity, Gordon-Conwell Theological Seminary (October 31, 2017); The **Joint Declaration on the Doctrine of Justification (JDDJ)**, October 31, 1999, is a document created, and agreed to, by the Catholic Church's Pontifical Council for Promoting Christian Unity (PCPCU) and the Lutheran World Federation in 1999, as a result of extensive ecumenical dialogue. It states that the churches now share "a common understanding of our justification by God's grace through faith in Christ." To the parties involved, this essentially resolves the 500-year-old conflict over the nature of justification which was at the root of the Protestant Reformation.

[66] Wikipedia, Orthodoxy, 1.

[67] Wikipedia, Arianism, Section 4.1, Beliefs, Struggles with Orthodoxy; Wikipedia, First Seven Ecumenical Councils, at Section 1.1, First Council of Nicaea (AD 325).

[68] Id.

God-bearer rather than Christ bearer, confirming the theological concept of union of God and man, both divine and human. The Council decreed that Jesus was one person (hypostasis) possessing two natures—both human and divine.[69] It also reconfirmed the Nicene Creed.[70] 4) The Council of Chalcedon (451) repudiated monophysitism (declaring Jesus had only one nature—divine) and adopted duophysitism and the formal definition of Hypostatic Union referring to the two natures of Christ (human and divine). [71] 5) The Second Council of Constantinople (553) was held at the direction of Emperor Justinian I to reunify spiritually the Byzantine Empire, which was in a religious schism caused by the Council of Chalcedon dealing with the divisive issue of the Hypostatic Union of Jesus (mostly the Oriental Church or Eastern Orthodoxy). Justinian I issued an edict that anathematized Nestorianism and the Three Chapters, which are the writings of Theodore of Mopsuestia (preached heresy against the original sin, and the Virgin Mary as Theotokos—Mother of God)[72], certain writings of Theodoret of Cyrus (continued to promote Nestorianism controversy about the Virgin Mary as the Mother of God (Theotokos) (Nestorianism), and whether Mary was the Christ-bearer and not the God-bearer), as well as the letter of Ibas of Edessa to Maris (anguish over extinguished Arianism (Jesus not consubstantial with God the Father) and praise of Theodoret's

---

[69] Wikipedia, Council of Ephesus, Sections 2.2, Theological Context and 4, Confirmation of the Council's Acts.

[70] Wikipedia, Ecumenical Council, at Section 5.1, First Ecumenical Councils.

[71] Wikipedia, First Seven Ecumenical Councils, at Section 1.4, Council of Chalcedon; Wikipedia, Council of Chalcedon.

[72] Wikipedia, Theodore of Mopsuestia, Section 1, Life and Work.

teachings).[73] 6) The Third Council of Constantinople (680–681) rejected monotheliticism and monoenerigism (belief that Jesus had two natures but only one will) which was considered and debated but rejected monotheliticism in favor of dyothetilism ("two natural wills with two natural energies, without division, alteration, separation or confusion").[74] 7) The Second Council of Nicaea (AD 787) rejected the Synod of Hieria and iconoclasm and ultimately restored the veneration and reverence of icons, and added the requirement that every altar contain a relic.[75]

These Councils have caused major schisms in the Christian Church. The Orthodox Church of the East accepts the first two councils. The Oriental Orthodox Church accepts the first three. Both the Eastern Orthodox Church and the Roman Catholic Church recognize as ecumenical the first seven councils. The Eastern Orthodox Church does not recognize any later synod or council, while the Roman Catholic Church continues to hold general councils of its College of Bishops to discuss matters of faith, morals, and theology in full communion with the Pope, considering them to be ecumenical. The Catholic Church recognizes a total of 21 councils.[76]

There are an estimated 260 million Eastern and Oriental Orthodox followers throughout the world.[77]

---

[73] Wikipedia, Three Chapter Controversy.

[74] Wikipedia, Monthelitiscism, Section 5, Condemnation of Monothelitism.

[75] Wikipedia, Second Council of Nicaea, Section 2, Proceedings; Wikipedia, First Seven Ecumenical Councils, Section 1.7, Second Council of Nicaea.

[76] Wikipedia, Ecumenical Councils, Section 1, Acceptance of Councils by Denomination; Wikipedia, Ecumenical Council, Section 5.1, List of ecumenical Councils and Section 6, Acceptance of Ecumenical Councils.

[77] Wikipedia, Orthodoxy by Country, Section 3, Statistics; "Pewforum: Christianity (2010)" (PDF). Retrieved 2014-05-14.

d. Judaism—Judaism has about 14.5–17 million followers worldwide.[78] Judaism is a unitarian monotheistic Abrahamic faith with the Torah (aka Pentateuch; first five books of the Old Testament handed down by Moses) as its foundational text.[79] The Torah contained 613 rules (roughly 1/3 proscriptive and 2/3 prescriptive). Only 369 are still applicable today. [80] It encompasses the religion, culture, and philosophy (e.g., government) of the Jewish tradition.[81] It is based on the original covenant God made with the Jewish people.[82] It is one of the oldest monotheistic religions, dating back over 3,000 years.[83] According to the Tanakh (Jewish Bible) God promised Abraham children to form a great nation.[84] The covenant with God is to love God and one another.[85] The most popular core tenants of the Jewish faith can be found in Maimonides (13 principles of faith formulated in the twelfth century) primarily extolling

---

[78] Wikipedia, Judaism, 1; The National Catholic Register, supra.

[79] Id; Shaye J.D. Cohen 1999 *The Beginnings of Jewishness: Boundaries, Varieties, Uncertainties*, Berkeley: University of California Press; 7

[80] Id, at Section 2.1, Jewish Legal Literature; *Danzinger, Eliezer. "How Many of the Torah's Commandments Still Apply?".* Chabad.org. Retrieved June 5, 2017.

[81] Id; *Jacobs, Louis "Judaism" In* Fred Skolnik. Encyclopaedia Judaica. **11** (2d ed.) (Farmington Hills, Mich.: Thomson Gale, 2007), *511. ISBN 978-0-02-865928-2. Judaism, the religion, philosophy, and way of life of the Jews.*

[82] Id; *"Knowledge Resources: Judaism". Berkley Center for Religion, Peace, and World Affairs. Retrieved 2011-11-22.*

[83] Id; David P Mindell. *The Evolving World.* (Harvard University Press. (30 June 2009), 224. *ISBN 978-0-674-04108-0.*

[84] Id, at Section 1.1, defining characteristics;

[85] Id; Leviticus 19:18: "'Do not seek revenge or bear a grudge against one of your people, but love your neighbor as yourself. I am the Lord"

the virtues of a single God and the Torah he handed down.[86] Sections 12 and 13 of Maimonides profess the coming of a Messiah and a life hereafter.[87] Rabbinic Judaism is the mainstream today, since the codification of the Jerusalem and Babylonian Talmuds (instruction) (collection of Rabbinic notes on the oral tradition [Mishnah] of the second century).[88]

Christianity was originally a sect of Second Temple Judaism, diverging in the first century.[89] Differences between Christianity and Judaism include whether Jesus Christ is the Jewish Messiah, atonement for sins, status of God's commandments given to Moses for Israel, and the nature of God.[90] Christians are currently working to reconcile with Jews in a common fight against antisemitism and radical terrorists.

Islam and Judaism both emanated from Abraham (Abrahamic religions).[91] Judaism stemmed from Abraham's son Isaac and Islam from his son Ishmael.[92] While both religions are monotheistic, Judaism does not believe Jesus or Muhammad are prophets.[93]

---

[86] Id, at Section 1.2, Core Tenants; *"Maimonides' 13 Foundations of Judaism"*. Mesora. "However if he rejects one of these fundamentals he leaves the nation and is a denier of the fundamentals and is called a heretic, a denier, etc."

[87] Id.

[88] Wikipedia, Jerusalem Talmud, 1.

[89] Id, at section 8.1, Christianity and Judaism.

[90] Id.

[91] Id, at Section 8.2, Islam and Judaism.

[92] Id.

[93] Id.

In the mid-twentieth century, most Jews have been expelled from Muslim countries. The rift has widened and solidified.[94] Radical factions of Islam, such as ISIS, Hezbollah, and Hamas, are trying to eliminate Judaism from the Middle East including Israel. Israel is in constant strife with the Palestinians regarding settlements in Israel.

e. **Islam**—With over 1.8 billion followers, it is the world's fastest growing religion and represents over 24% of the world's population.[95] Islam is a unitarian monotheistic Abrahamic religion holding that there is only one God (Allah)[96] and that Muhammad was a messenger from God.[97]

The Islamic faith was founded by Muhammad (born AD 570). He claimed he received a revelation from the angel Gabriel concerning one God, *Allah*, and a command to commit to Allah. Muhammad tried to convert his idolatrous fellow citizens in Mecca, but they expelled him. Muhammad fled to Medina in AD 622. He later returned to Mecca in AD 630 and

---

[94] Id; "Why Jews Fled the Arab Countries". *Middle East Forum*. Retrieved on July 28, 2013; Shumsky, Dmitry. (September 9, 2012) "Recognize Jews as refugees from Arab countries". *Haaretz*. Retrieved on July 28, 2013; Meir, Esther. (October 10, 2012) "The truth about the expulsion". 'Haaretz. *Retrieved on July 28, 2013.*

[95] Wikipedia, Islam, 1; *"Why Muslims are the world's fastest-growing religious group". Pew Research Center. April 6, 2017. Retrieved May, 11 2017;* Burke, Daniel *"The world's fastest-growing religion is .."(CNN, April 4, 2015.* Retrieved 18 April 2015; The National Catholic Register, supra.

[96] Id; www.quran.com.

[97] Id; Esposito, John L. "Islam. Overview". In John L. Esposito. The Oxford Encyclopedia of the Islamic World. Oxford: Oxford University Press,*2009). Profession of Faith [...] affirms Islam's absolute monotheism and acceptance of Muḥammad as the messenger of God, the last and final prophet.*

conquered it. He cleansed the central shrine of all the idols and made it the center of worship of Allah.[98]

The fundamental Muslim beliefs are contained in six doctrines that every Muslim must believe in:[99]
1. God is one. He is transcendent and unknowable yet somehow personal. He is compassionate and merciful but can become angry. He is the almighty creator and predestinator of everything.
2. Angels and *jinn*. Supernatural beings that influence human affairs.
3. God's prophets and messengers. Prophets are distinct from messengers, in that they brought a book from God. Muhammed is the greatest of the last of the prophets because he brought the book called the Quran. No new prophet will appear after him.
4. The Books of God. These include the Jewish Torah, David's Psalms, the New Testament, and the Quran. The Quran is the last and, therefore, the final and best word from God.
5. Judgment day when all will be judged according to their works. Sin is a moral, social, and ceremonial issue. It is seen as a weakness in humans, not as in the Bible, but a complete moral corruption making a person unable to please God by their efforts. So those who have done sufficient good works may enter a sensual Paradise. Those who haven't are thrown into a hell of fire.
6. Inch'allah–the will of God. God is absolutely sovereign, and whatever he decrees must come to pass. Humanity's task is merely to submit to the will of God.

---

[98] YWAM 50th Anniversary Study Bible (NIV), YWAM Publishing, (2010), 1355.

[99] Id, at 1355-56.

The primary scriptures of Islam are the Quran. They are viewed as the verbatim word of God.[100] Muslims believe that Islam is the combined revelations of Adam, Abraham, Moses, and Jesus.[101] It is the final and unaltered word of God.[102] Like other Abrahamic religions, Islam teaches that there will be a final judgment, and the righteous will gain Heaven and the unrighteous Hell.[103] There are two sects to Islam – Sunni (75–90%) and Shia (10–20%).[104]

Religious practices are based on the Five Pillars of Islam, which are obligatory acts of worship.[105] The Five Sunni Pillars are: 1) Shahada: Faith–The central confession of faith. There is only one God, Allah, and, Muhammed is his prophet; 2) Salat: Prayer–five daily prayers facing Mecca; 3) Zakat: Charity–giving alms and helping the needy or poor; 4) Sawm: Fasting–obligatory dawn to dusk during Ramadan to seek nearness to God and forgiveness for sins; 5) Hajj: Pilgrimage to Mecca–at least once in a lifetime as an expression of devotion to God.[106] The Five Shia Pillars are: 1) Tawhid–monotheism and one God, 2) Adl–belief in the justice of God, 3) Nubuwwah–prophethood, 4) Imamah–succession to the

---

[100]Id.

[101]Id; *"People of the Book", Islam: Empire of Faith.* PBS. Retrieved December 18, 2010.

[102]Id: *Bennett, Clinton (2010). Interpreting the Qur'an: a guide for the uninitiated. Continuum International Publishing Group. p. 101. ISBN 978-0-8264-9944-8.*

[103]Id;. *Esposito, John L "Islam. Overview" (2009).*

[104]Id; *Harney, John "How Do Sunni and Shia Islam Differ?".* The New York Times, January 3, 2016). Retrieved January 4, 2016; Almukhtar, Sarah; Peçanha, Sergio; Wallace, Tim *"Behind Stark Political Divisions, a More Complex Map of Sunnis and Shiites".* (The New York Times,(January 5, 2016). Retrieved January 6, 2016.

[105]Id; John L. Esposito (2009), supra, In John L. Esposito, The Oxford Encyclopedia of the Islamic World. Oxford: Oxford University Press, 17.

[106]Wikipedia, Five Pillars of Islam, 1.

Muhammad, and 5) Mi'ad–the Day of Judgment and Resurrection. In addition, there are 10 practices for Shia Muslims: 1) Salat, 2) Sawm, 3) Zakat, 4) Khums–paying 20% of income to the Imams and then indirectly to the poor, 5) Hajj, 6) Jihad–struggle and proselytizing, 7) enjoining good, 8) forbidding wrong, 9) Tawallah–expressing love towards good, and 10) Tabarra–expressing disassociation and hatred toward evil.[107]

Sharia law is the religious law forming part of the Islamic tradition and comes from the Quran and Hadith.[108] Areas of Sharia overlap with Western notion of law while others tend toward living according to God's will.[109] In Islam there is no separation between church and state.

Sunnis believe that they are heirs and successors of Muhammad through the first four caliphs.[110] They follow the Quran and Hadith.[111] Shias believe that Muhammad appointed his son in law, Ali ibn Abi Talib, the first Imam, as his successor, trumping the four prior caliphs recognized by the Sunni's.[112]

Muslims believe Jesus was a great prophet, but they do not believe in Jesus' crucifixion or resurrection. Instead they believe it was someone else who died on the cross and that he escaped death, but that he did eventually ascend into heaven. Muslims believe that Muhammad was the last and greatest of all the prophets.

---

[107] Id, at Sections 1, Pillars of Sunni Islam and 2, Pillars of Shia Islam.

[108] Wikipedia, Islam, at Section 4, Law and Jurisprudence; *"British & World English: sharia"*. (Oxford: Oxford. University Press). Retrieved December 4, 2015.

[109] Id.

[110] Id, at Section 7, Denominations, Sunni.

[111] Id.

[112] Id, at Section 7, Denominations, Shia.

f. Mormonism–15.8 million followers.[113] A unitarian sect, founded in the 1820s by Joseph Smith, who was searching for the truth and had visions, causing him to claim he received gold plates from Heaven interpreting Scripture as a chronicle of the indigenous peoples of the Americas in their dealings with God.[114] The largest group is the LDS (Latter Day Saints), who accepted Brigham Young and believe in plural marriage (polygamy).[115] These beliefs and practices have been discarded and no longer hold true for this faith, causing the LDS church to separate from mainstream Mormonism.[116] LDS believes in the Old and New Testaments but believe errors were introduced and that the Book of Mormon corrected them. [117] Mormonism

---

[113]Wikipedia, The church of Jesus Christ of Latter-Day Saints Membership Statistics, 1.

[114]Wikipedia, Mormonism, 1.

[115]Id, at Section 1.

[116]Id, at Section 4.1, Mainstream Mormon Theology ; Examples of organizations that do not recognize Mormonism as Christian include:
• Luther Seminary (*Granquist, Mark A. luthersem.edu (PDF), Lay School of Religion, Luther Seminary, March 7, 2011.* http://www.luthersem.edu/lifelong_learning/layschool/handouts/New%20and%20Old%20Religions%20Slides%20Session%204.pdf ;
 • Midwestern Baptist Theological Seminary (*"News & Resources", mbts.edu, October 20, 2011* .
 • Southern Baptist Theological Seminary (*Mohler, Albert (n.d.), "Is Mormonism Christian?", christianity.com, Salem Web Network* .
See also: Christian counterculture movement.

[117]Id, at Section 2.5; *Encyclopedia of Mormonism*, Macmillan 1992, pp. 106-107; *Teachings of the Prophet Joseph Smith, Deseret Book, 1976 [1938], 9–10, 32.7*

is outside the umbrella of the Christian faith.[118] They believe that God the Father is supreme over other spirits and over men and women, who can, however, become exalted and inherit all that God has to offer and can become joint heirs of Jesus Christ and like unto equal gods.[119]

g. **Jehovah's Witnesses**—A unitarian belief distinct from the Christian faith. They number about 8.3 million.[120] They deny the Trinity because they believe in only one true or mighty God who is the Father.[121] They emanated from a Bible Study Movement in the 1870s.[122] They believe their denomination is a revival of the teachings of the first-century Christians. They believe in continuing revelations, which are published in the Watch Tower publication.[123] They reject the Trinity and the concept of immortality of the soul. They reject military service and refuse blood transfusions and some medical treatments.[124]

---

[118] Id, at Section 3.1, Relation to Mainstream Christianity; Examples of organizations that do not recognize Mormonism as Christian include:
- Luther Seminary (*Granquist, Mark A, luthersem.edu (PDF)*, Lay School of Religion, Luther Seminary (March 7, 2011)
http://www.luthersem.edu/lifelong_learning/layschool/handouts/New%20and%20Old%20Religions%20Slides%20Session%204.pdf .
  - Midwestern Baptist Theological Seminary (*"News & Resources", mbts.edu, October 20, 2011* |contribution= ignored (help));
  - Southern Baptist Theological Seminary (*Mohler, Albert (n.d.), "Is Mormonism Christian?", christianity.com, Salem Web Network* .
  See also: Christian countercult movement

[119] Id, at Section 2.1, Nature of God.

[120] Wikipedia, Jehovah's Witnesses, 1.

[121] Horn, Trent, supra at 62.

[122] Wikipedia, Jehovah's Witnesses, 1.

[123] Id, at Section 3.1.

[124] Id, at 1.

h. **Sikhs**—A monotheistic religion, founded in the Punjab (modern-day Pakistan) ca. AD 1500 by the Guru Nanak, which refuses to recognize the Hindu caste system or the Brahmanical priesthood and forbids magic, idolatry, and pilgrimages. It has approximately 26 million followers.[125] "The fundamental beliefs of Sikhism, articulated in the sacred scripture Guru Granth Sahib include faith and meditation on the name of the one creator, divine unity and equality of all humankind, engaging in selfless service , striving for social justice for the benefit and prosperity of all, and honest conduct and livelihood while living a householder's life."[126] "Sikhism is based on the spiritual teachings of Guru Nanak, the first Guru (1469 – 1539),[127] and the nine Sikh gurus that succeeded him. The Tenth Guru, Guru Gobind Singh, named the Sikh scripture Guru Granth Sahib as his successor, terminating the line of human Gurus and making the scripture the eternal, religious spiritual guide for Sikhs."[128] "Sikhism rejects claims that any particular religious tradition has a monopoly on absolute truth."[129] "In

---

[125]The National Catholic Register; Wikipedia, Sikhism.

[126]Wikipedia, Sikhism, 1; *Sewa Singh Kalsi. Sikhism. Chelsea House, Philadelphia. pp. 41–50; William Owen Cole; Piara Singh Sambhi (1995). The Sikhs: Their Religious Beliefs and Practices. Sussex Academic Press. p. 200; Teece, Geoff (2004). Sikhism:Religion in focus. Black Rabbit Books. p. 4. ISBN 978-1-58340-469-0.*

[127]Singh, Patwant; The Sikhs.(Alfred A Knopf Publishing, 2000), 17. ISBN 0-375-40728-6.

[128]Fenech, Louis and WH McLeod Historical Dictionary of Sikhism, 3rd Edition, (Rowman & Littlefield, 2014), ISBN 978-1442236004, pp. 17, 84-85; William James, God's Plenty: Religious Diversity in Kingston,(McGill Queens University Press, 2011), ISBN 978-0773538894, pages 241–242; Mann, Gurinder Singh, *The Making of Sikh Scripture. (United States: Oxford University Press, 2001), 21–25, 123–124. ISBN 978-0-19-513024-9.*

[129]*Id.*

Sikhism, the concept of 'God' is Waheguru considered Nirankar (shapeless), akal (timeless), and Alakh Niranjan (invisible). The Sikh scripture begins with Ik Onkar (ੴ), which refers to the "formless one," and understood in the Sikh tradition as monotheistic unity of God. Sikhism is classified as an Indian religion along with Buddhism, Hinduism, and Jainism, given its geographical origin and its sharing some concepts with them.[130] "God" in Sikhism is known as Ik Onkar, the One Supreme Reality or the all-pervading spirit (which is taken to mean God). "Sikhism regards God as the true king, the king of all kings, the one who dispenses justice through the law of karma, a retributive model and divine grace."[131] "This spirit has no gender in Sikhism, though translations may present it as masculine. It is also *Akaal Purkh* (beyond time and space) and *Nirankar* (without form). In addition, Nanak wrote that there are many worlds on which it has created life."[132] "Guru Nanak's teachings are founded not on a final destination of heaven or hell but on a spiritual union with the Akal, which results in salvation or *Jivanmutka* (liberation whilst alive), a concept also found in

---

[130] Pashaura Singh in The Oxford Handbook of Sikh Studies (Editors: Pashaura Singh, Louis E. Fenech), (Oxford University Press, 2014). ISBN 978-0199699308, page 227; Doniger, Wendy (1999). Merriam-Webster's Encyclopedia of World Religions. Merriam-Webster. p. 500. ISBN 978-0-87779-044-0.; Torkel Brekke (2014). Gregory M. Reichberg and Henrik Syse, ed. Religion, War, and Ethics: A Sourcebook of Textual Traditions. Cambridge University Press. p. 672. ISBN 978-1-139-95204-0. ; Quote: "As an Indian religion, Sikhism affirms transmigration, the continued rebirth after death..."; Sikhism"", Encyclopedia Britannica; Quote: "Sikhism, Indian religion founded in the Punjab in the late 15th century."; See also Classification of Religions, Encyclopedia Britannica.

[131] Chanchreek, Jain Encyclopaedia of Great Festivals. Shree Publishers & Distributors, (2007), 142. ISBN 9788183291910.; *Dugga, Kartar*). Maharaja Ranjit Singh: The Last to Lay Arms. Abhinav Publications, (2001), 33. ISBN 9788170174103.

[132] Mayled, John, Sikhism (Heinemann Press,2002), 16. ISBN 0-435-33627-4.

Hinduism. Guru Gobind Singh makes it clear that human birth is obtained with great fortune, therefore one needs to be able to make the most of this life. Sikhs believe in reincarnation and karma concepts found in Hinduism and Buddhism."[133]

2. **Polytheistic Religions**[134]—Multiple god–centered; individual gods or deities serve different purposes through forces of nature or ancestry; examples are found in Greek and ancient Roman history; types of deities include: 1) creator, 2) culture, 3) death, 4) life-death-rebirth, 5) love, 6) mother goddess; 7) political, 8) sky, 9) solar, 10) trickster (person who cheats or deceives people), 11) water, and 12) music, arts, science, farming, and other endeavors. [135]

Examples of present-day polytheism include:

a. **Buddhism**—Indian religion following the teachings of Buddha.[136] It reaches back to 450 BCE or earlier,[137] and has approximately 500 million followers worldwide. [138]

---

[133]Takhar, Opinderjit (2005). Sikh Identity: An Exploration Of Groups Among Sikhs. Ashgate Publishing, Ltd. p. 143 ISBN 9780754652021; Grewal, JS (1998). The Sikhs of the Punjab. United Kingdom: Cambridge University Press. pp. 25–36. ISBN 0521637643; Chahal, Amarjit Singh (December 2011). "Concept of Reincarnation in Guru Nanak's Philosophy" (PDF). Understanding Sikhism – The Research Journal. **13** (1–2): 52–59. Retrieved 29 November 2013.

[134]Wikipedia, Polytheism, 1-11

[135]Id, at Section 4, Types of Deities.

[136]Wikipedia, Buddhism, 1.

[137]Id, at Section 6.1, Timeline.

[138]Id, at Section 7.1, Demographics; Pew Research Center. "Global Religious Landscape: Buddhists". Pew Research Center; The National Catholic Register, supra

Founded according legendary accounts of Siddhartha Gautama (Buddha), written centuries after his death, Buddhism was conceived to deal with the distressing human suffering he experienced. About 530 BC, Gautama experienced an "enlightenment" during a time of meditation under a Bodhi tree. This gave him the name of Buddha. From this enlightenment he developed "Four Noble Truths:"[139]

1. Suffering is universal.
2. The cause of suffering is desire or craving.
3. The cure for suffering is to eliminate desire.
4. Craving is eliminated by following the "Eight-fold path."

The Eight-Fold Path consists of:
1) Right viewpoint; 2) right aspiration; 3) right speech; 4) right behavior; 5) right occupation; 6) right effort; 7) right mindfulness; and 8) right meditation.

The key to "rightness" is accepting our given place in life and not striving for something beyond it. This preserves social harmony and puts an end to desire, the source of suffering.

Buddhism's important beliefs are like Hinduism, monism—all reality is ultimately one. Through *karma* and reincarnation, good works, and self-control, the final enlightenment (*Nirvana*) can be reached. However, none is ever sure if they have done enough to warrant Nirvana.

Buddhism differs from Hinduism in two aspects: 1) no caste system, and 2) no formal opinion as to whether or not there is a God of any kind whatsoever. This religion concerns itself with humanity and the human condition rather than with a god. Over time two main streams of Buddhism developed. Theravada Buddhism of Sri Lanka, Burma, Cambodia, and Thailand, which teaches that the Buddha was an enlightened man who through

---

[139] YWAM 50th Anniversary Study Bible, supra at 1354–55.

Religiosity by Generation–Many Different Religions and Worldviews

self-effort taught others to reach *nirvana* through monastic withdrawal and the practice of its disciplines. Mahayana Buddhism views Buddha and Bodhisattvas (future Buddhas) as divine beings who can save if one has faith in them.[140]

As for general practices and beliefs, higher beings are designated as gods, Devas; Buddha pioneered the path to enlightenment but is not worshipped but merely reflected on; statues of the Buddha are used to reflect on qualities that are important. There is no creator, and the Buddha rejected the idea that there is a permanent, personal, fixed, omniscient deity. This links into the core concept of impermanence.[141] Belief in the cycle of rebirth and Karma, i.e., good deeds produce good seeds and bad deeds produce bad seeds.[142] This eventually leads the state of liberation–Nirvana.[143] They believe in an afterlife.[144]

b. **Shintoism**—Originates with the Japanese; founded sixth century AD; 100 million Japanese followers[145]; worships deities called "Kami" and prays to the deities of Shinto as a form of Buddha.[146] Shinto gods are spirits that are everywhere in nature and also in men. Symbolism indicates that there are over 8 million gods in Shinto. Shinto spirits live in nature (form of animism) and ancestors. Shinto deals mostly with this life and issues such as personal salvation are not discussed. Souls

---

[140]Id.

[141]Wikipedia, Polytheism, 1-11.

[142]Wikipedia, Buddhism, Section 2.2, Rebirth and Karma.

[143]Id, at Section 2.3, Liberation.

[144]Wikipedia, Buddhism, at Section 3.2, Path to Liberation, Eightfold Path Matrix

[145]Mizumura, Michiko, Chapter 18, Revealing the One True God to the Polytheistic Shinto Culture, World Religions and Cults, June 23, 2017, 2.

[146]Id.

go to an underworld.[147] There are over 80,000 Shinto shrines in Japan.[148] Shinto and Buddhism have been syncretized (attempt to amalgamate or reconcile differing things, especially religious beliefs, cultural elements, or schools of thought).[149]

c. **Confucianism**—Developed by the Chinese philosopher Confucius, who lived between 551 and 479 BCE; the core is humanistic relying on family and social harmony. Concern is this worldly. Followers number about 5.3 million.[150] Human beings are basically good, teachable, and capable of perfection. They believe in righteousness and acting every day in accordance with the laws of heaven.[151] Today they follow qualities such as filial piety, humanity, justice, etiquette, ethics, and morals.[152] Unity between self and heaven (Tian).[153] Tian can be compared to Hindu gods.[154]

d. **Hinduism**—Hinduism is an Indian way of life and ancient faith going back about 3,500 years to 5,500 BCE, according to some scholars. It is called the oldest religion in the world. It is a synthesis of various traditions and cultures.[155] Hindus venerate

---

[147] Id, at 16.

[148] Id, at 3.

[149] Id, at 12.

[150] Google Sites, Confucianism, Demographics and Geography, 1.

[151] Wikipedia, Confucianism, 1.

[152] Id.

[153] Id, at 2.

[154] Id, at 3.

[155] Wikipedia, Hinduism, 1; Hinduism is variously defined as a "religion," "set of religious beliefs and practices," "religious tradition," "a way of life." Sharma (2003), 12–13. For a discussion on the topic, see: "Establishing the boundaries" in Flood (2008), 1–17.

deities in the form of idols; worship entails communicating "... with formless, abstract divinity which creates, sustains and dissolves creation."

Hinduism teaches monism—everything in the universe is ultimately one. This is a god or *Brahman*. This divine unity is not a person. *Brahman* is the impersonal, ultimate reality. Each soul is a part of Brahman. Not only humans have eternal souls. All life is divine. This means a person can be reincarnated as an animal. Central to Hinduism is the concept of reincarnation—that is, the soul is reborn after death, probably millions of times. The universe and individual are *maya*—an illusion, so the purpose of life is to finally escape back into reality, the impersonal *Brahman*.[156]

Hinduism has no particular written special revelation from God, but there are essential scriptures such as Vedas containing philosophical reflections and myths of the gods. They have essentially the same authority to Hindus as the Bible does to Christians.[157] "Prominent themes in Hindu beliefs include the four Purusarthas, the proper goals or aims of human life, namely Dharma (ethics/duties), Artha (prosperity/work), Kama (desires/passions), and Moksha (liberation/freedom/salvation);[158] karma (action, intent, and consequences), Samsara (cycle of rebirth), and the various Yogas (paths or practices

---

[156]YWAM 50th Anniversary Study Bible, supra, at 1355.

[157]Id.

[158]Id; *Bilimoria; et al., eds. (2007). Indian Ethics: Classical Traditions and Contemporary Challenges. p. 103.* CS1 maint: Explicit use of et al. () See also *Koller, John). "Puruṣārtha as Human Aims".* Philosophy East and West, (1968*). 18 (4): 315–319. doi:10.2307/1398408. JSTOR 1398408; Flood, Gavin "The Meaning and Context of the Puruṣārthas". In Lipner, Julius J. The Bhagavadgītā for Our Times.* (Oxford University Press, 1997), pp. 11–27. ISBN 978-0195650396.

to attain moksha)."[159] Absolute truth is fully personal as in the Judeo-Christian tradition. Their belief is in reincarnation as devas, with enough good karma, if they led good lives.[160] Teaching is done by gurus, avatars, sages, and saints.[161] Followers number about 1.15 billion.[162]

e. **Paganism**—Origin in Middle Age Europe—Neopaganism derives from various historical pagan beliefs of premodern Europe. Term used by Christians in the fourth century AD by early Christians for populations within the Roman Empire who practiced polytheistic religions. Another term is gentile. Most pagans are polytheistic, pantheistic, or animistic.[163] Largest sect is Wiccan. Estimated 1 million followers in the US with about 300,000 elsewhere throughout the world.[164]

f. **Animism**—Common to most tribal peoples of the world and greatly influenced popular Hinduism, Buddhism, and Islam, as well as Christianity. Most followers of tribal religions believe in a creator god who formed the universe in the mythical past. He is unconcerned with humans, but there is a promise that somehow they will be brought back to their god. These are spirit worshippers. There are three spirits in animism:

---

[159] Id; *Klostermaier, Klaus A Survey of Hinduism (3rd ed.).* (State University of New York Press, 2007), 46–52, 76–77. ISBN 978-0791470824.

[160] Wikipedia, Polytheism, 7.

[161] Wikipedia, Hinduism, at Section 4.5, Authority.

[162] Id, *"Christianity 2015: Religious Diversity and Personal Contact" (PDF). gordonconwell.edu. January 2015. Retrieved May, 5, 2015;* The National Catholic Register, supra.

[163] Wikipedia, Paganism, 1.

[164] Wikipedia, Modern Paganism, Demographics.

1. Ancestral–dead ancestors are believed to be still present and still concerned about the welfare of family and tribe.
2. Nature Spirits–associated with natural phenomena (thunder, storms, droughts) and inanimate objects (rocks, rivers, trees).
3. Animals–every animal has a spirit.

Fear is the constant motivator. These spirits must be constantly appeased so they don't get angry. They can be called on to do good or evil toward other persons. Protection is afforded by bracelets and the local witch doctor. Sin and guilt are understood in the social and ceremonial context. Humanity is seen as part of the circle of life linking all creation, which extends to ancestral gods who may be mythical men taking the form of animals.[165]

---

[165] YWAM 50th Anniversary Bible, supra, 1356.

3. **Agnosticism and Atheism**—Atheism in its broadest form is the absence of a belief in entities.[166] Atheism can also mean the rejection of belief that any gods exist.[167] It can also mean that

---

[166]Wikipedia, Atheism, 1; *Harvey, Van A. Agnosticism and Atheism,* in Flynn 2007, 35: "The terms *ATHEISM* and *AGNOSTICISM* lend themselves to two different definitions. The first takes the privative *a* both before the Greek *theos* (divinity) and *gnosis* (to know) to mean that atheism is simply the absence of belief in the gods and agnosticism is simply lack of knowledge of some specified subject matter. The second definition takes atheism to mean the explicit denial of the existence of gods and agnosticism as the position of someone who, because the existence of gods is unknowable, suspends judgment regarding them ... The first is the more inclusive and recognizes only two alternatives: Either one believes in the gods or one does not. Consequently, there is no third alternative, as those who call themselves agnostics sometimes claim. Insofar as they lack belief, they are really atheists. Moreover, since absence of belief is the cognitive position in which everyone is born, the burden of proof falls on those who advocate religious belief. The proponents of the second definition, by contrast, regard the first definition as too broad because it includes uninformed children along with aggressive and explicit atheists. Consequently, it is unlikely that the public will adopt it."; *Simon Blackburn, ed. "atheism". The Oxford Dictionary of Philosophy (2008 ed.). (Oxford University Press, 2008). Retrieved 2013-11-21.* Either the lack of belief that there exists a god, or the belief that there exists none. Sometimes thought itself to be more dogmatic than mere agnosticism, although atheists retort that everyone is an atheist about most gods, so they merely advance one step further.

[167]Id; Nielsen 2013: "Instead of saying that an atheist is someone who believes that it is false or probably false that there is a God, a more adequate characterization of atheism consists in the more complex claim that to be an atheist is to be someone who rejects belief in God for the following reasons ... : for an anthropomorphic God, the atheist rejects belief in God because it is false or probably false that there is a God; for a nonanthropomorphic God ... because the concept of such a God is either meaningless, unintelligible, contradictory, incomprehensible, or incoherent; for the God portrayed by some modern or contemporary theologians or philosophers ... because the concept of God in question is such that it merely masks an atheistic substance—e.g., "God" is just another name for love, or ... a symbolic term for moral ideals."

there are no deities.[168] Atheism is contrasted with theism, which believes that there is at least one god.[169] Atheism first arose in the sixteenth century AD.[170] Arguments supporting beliefs in atheism range from philosophical to social.[171] The typical rationales for not believing in deities include 1) the supposed lack of empirical data,[172] 2) prevalence of evil (God and evil cannot coexist),[173] 3) inconsistent revelations (monotheistic faiths, e.g., Christian, Muslim, Judaism, and polytheistic faiths),[174] 4) doctrine of falsifiability–can't reject something that cannot be falsified–questioning of hypotheses,[175] and 5) argument from non-belief (inconsistency between the

---

[168] Id; Rowe 1998: "As commonly understood, atheism is the position that affirms the nonexistence of God. So an atheist is someone who disbelieves in God, whereas a theist is someone who believes in God. Another meaning of 'atheism' is simply nonbelief in the existence of God, rather than positive belief in the nonexistence of God. ... an atheist, in the broader sense of the term, is someone who disbelieves in every form of deity, not just the God of traditional Western theology."

[169] Id; *Oxford English Dictionary (2nd ed.). 1989. Belief in a deity, or deities, as opposed to atheism*; Smart, J. J. C. Zalta, Edward N., ed. *"Atheism and Agnosticism". The Stanford Encyclopedia of Philosophy (Spring 2013 Edition).*

[170] Id; *Wootton, David "1. New Histories of Atheism". In Hunter, Michael; Wootton, David. Atheism from the Reformation to the Enlightenment* (Oxford: Clarendon Press, 1992). ISBN 0-19822736-1.

[171] Id; *Various authors. "Logical Arguments for Atheism". The Secular Web Library. Internet Infidels. Retrieved 2012-10-02.*

[172] Id; *Various authors. "Logical Arguments for Atheism". The Secular Web Library. Internet Infidels. Retrieved 2012-10-02.; Shook, John R. "Skepticism about the Supernatural" (PDF). Retrieved 2012-10-02*

[173] Id; Wikipedia, Problem of Evil, 1)

[174] Id; Wikipedia, Problem with Inconsistent Revelations, 1)

[175] Id; Wikipedia, Falsifiability, 1.

existence of a God and a world that fails to recognize Him, i.e., if God existed everyone would believe in God).[176]

Atheism and agnosticism have been treated both as compatible[177] and incompatible concepts.[178] Atheism is coherent with some religious and spiritual belief systems, including Hinduism, Buddhism, and Neopagan movements such as Wicca.[179]

> Axiological, or constructive, atheism rejects the existence of gods in favor of a "higher absolute," such as humanity. This form of atheism favors humanity as the absolute source of ethics and values and permits individuals to resolve moral problems without resorting to God. Marx and Freud used this argument to convey messages of liberation, full development, and unfettered happiness.[180] One

---

[176] Id; Wikipedia, Argument from Non-Belief, 1.

[177] Argument from Non-Belief, supra, Section 1.1, Definitions and Types, Range; Holland, Aaron. Agnosticism, in Flynn 2007, p. 34: "It is important to note that this interpretation of agnosticism is compatible with theism or atheism, since it is only asserted that *knowledge* of God's existence is unattainable."

[178] Id; *"Atheism". Encyclopædia Britannica Concise. Merriam Webster. Retrieved December 15, 2011. Critique and denial of metaphysical beliefs in God or divine beings. Unlike agnosticism, which leaves open the question of whether there is a God, atheism is a positive denial. It is rooted in an array of philosophical systems.*

[179] Id, at Section 2.5, Atheism, Religions and Spirituality; *Johnson, Philip; et al. Claydon, David; et al., eds. Religious and Non-Religious Spirituality in the Western World ("New Age"). A New Vision, A New Heart, A Renewed Call.* **2**. (William Carey Library, *2005*), 194. ISBN 978-0-878-08364-0. Although Neo-Pagans share common commitments to nature and spirit there is a diversity of beliefs and practices ... Some are atheists, others are polytheists (several gods exist), some are pantheists (all is God) and others are panentheists (all is in God).

[180] Id: Zdybicka, Zofia J, "Atheism" In Maryniarczyk, Andrzej, Universal Encyclopedia of Philosophy. **1**. Polish Thomas Aquinas Association, (2005). Retrieved April 9, 2011.

of the most common criticisms of atheism has been to the contrary—that denying the existence of a god leads to moral relativism,[181] leaving one with no moral or ethical foundation[182] or renders life meaningless and miserable.[183]

It is difficult to quantify the number of atheists in the world. It is believed they number somewhere between 500 million to 1.1 billion.[184] In the US alone, 11.1% of individuals surveyed in a 2004 survey claimed they did not believe in God.[185] According to the 2014 World Values Survey, 3.1% of Americans self-identified as atheists and 4% as agnostics, and 11.1% said they did not believe in a God, while 15.8% identified as "nones."[186] By 2015, that number of atheists had risen to 5%.[187]

---

[181] Id.; *Gleeson, David (August 10, 2006). "Common Misconceptions About Atheists and Atheism". Retrieved 2013-11-21.*

[182] Id; *Gleeson, David (August 10, 2006). "Common Misconceptions About Atheists and Atheism". Retrieved 2013-11-21.*

[183] Id; Smith 1979, p. 275. "Perhaps the most common criticism of atheism is the claim that it leads inevitably to moral bankruptcy."

[184] Id, at Section 7, Demographics; *Zuckerman, Phil, "Atheism: Contemporary Rates and Patterns"*, (Cambridge Companion to Atheism, 2007), 947–66, doi:10.1017/CCOL0521842700.004; Joas, Hans; Wiegandt, Klaus, eds. *Secularization and the World Religions, (Liverpool University Press, 2010), 122 (footnote 1).* ISBN 978-1-84631-187-1. OL 25285702M. Retrieved 2012-04-18.; *Zuckerman, Phil "Atheism: Contemporary Rates and Patterns",* (Cambridge Companion to Atheism, 2007), 47–66, doi:10.1017/CCOL0521842700.004

[185] Id; "WVS Database". World Values Survey. Institute for Comparative Survey Research. *March 2015.*

[186] Id; "WVS Database", supra.

[187] Id; America's Changing Religious Landscape, Pew Research Center, 12 May 2015; Wikipedia, Demographics of Atheism; *Zuckerman, Phil "Atheism: Contemporary Rates and Patterns",* (Cambridge Companion to Atheism, 2007), 47–66, doi:10.1017/CCOL0521842700.004.

Unaffiliated Make Up Growing Share Across Generations

% of each generation that identifies <u>current</u> religion as atheist, agnostic or nothing in particular

	2007	2014	Change
Silent generation (b. 1928-1945)	9	11	+2
Baby Boomers (b.1946-1964)	14	17	+3
Generation X (b. 1965-1980)	19	23	+4
Older Millennials (b. 1981-1989)	25	34	+9
Younger Millennials (b. 1990-1996)	n/a	36	n/a

2014 Religious Landscape Study, conducted June 4-Sept. 30, 2014. All changes are statistically significant.

PEW RESEARCH CENTER

[188]

4. **Wiccan/Witchcraft**—Wiccan is a duotheistic faith created by Gerald Gardner, worshipping the Lord and Lady of the Isles (names are oath bound). Emphasizes duality and the cycle of nature.[189] Some consider Wiccans and Druids to be Pagans.[190]

5. **Satanism**—Theistic Satanists venerate Satan as a supernatural deity, viewing him not as omnipotent but rather as patriarch. In contrast, atheistic Satanists regard Satan as merely a symbol

---

[188] Id; America's Changing Religious Landscape, Pew Research Center, 12 May 2015; Wikipedia, Demographics of Atheism; Zuckerman, Phil *"Atheism: Contemporary Rates and Patterns"*,(Cambridge Companion to Atheism,2007) supra at 47–66, doi:10.1017/CCOL0521842700.004.

[189] Wikipedia, Polytheism, p 8.

[190] Wikipedia, Paganism.

of certain human traits.[191] The Church of Satan was formed in the United States in 1966 by Anton LaVey.[192] A number of religious studies scholars have described LaVey's Satanism as a form of "self-religion" or "self-spirituality."[193] It rejects the opportunity for God's salvation; truth is what Satan says it is; good vs. evil; carnal pleasures vs. spiritual restraint. Satanists become gods unto themselves.[194]

---

[191] Wikipedia, Satanism, p 1.

[192] Id, at Section 4.2.1.

[193] Id.

[194] Id.

CHAPTER III

Impact of Culture/Sociology On Religious Worldview

*"**Culture**—set of patterns of human activity within a community or social group and the symbolic structures that give such activity significance. Customs, laws, dress, architectural style, social standards, religious beliefs, and traditions are all examples of cultural elements."*[195]

Cultures are most commonly known by geographic, geopolitical, and ethnic regions–African, Asian, Indian, Middle Eastern.[196] Cultures can also be defined by cultural groups–communities and societies–defined by some common relationship.[197] And, of course, cultures can be defined by common interests known as subcultures.[198]

"In the United States, cultural studies focuses largely on the study of popular culture, that is, on the social meanings of mass-produced consumer and leisure goods. .... Cultural studies

---

[195] Wikipedia, Outline of Culture, p 1

[196] Id, at Section 5.

[197] Id, at Section 1.

[198] Id, at Section 3.

in this sense, then, can be viewed as a limited concentration scoped on the intricacies of consumerism, which belongs to a wider culture sometimes referred to as 'Western civilization' or 'globalism.'"[199]

"Culture in the sociological field can be defined as the ways of thinking, the ways of acting, and the material objects that together shape a people's way of life. Culture can be any of two types: non-material culture or material culture. Non-material culture refers to the non-physical ideas that individuals have about their culture, including values, belief systems, rules, norms, morals, language, organizations, and institutions, while material culture is the physical evidence of a culture in the objects and architecture they make or have made. The term tends to be relevant only in archeological and anthropological studies, but it specifically means all material evidence which can be attributed to culture, past or present."[200]

Most monotheistic, including Christian, services and polytheistic worship services around the world will reflect the local culture. Cultural elements permeate the Christian service, including song, dance, and nuances of worship. It is important to note that culture is very much a part of the celebration of God's glory. I believe and contend in this case that this is exactly what God wants of us—cultural expression celebrating the uniqueness of each individual and cultural group.

Sociology—a more general concept, defining multiple outside forces and trends that affect people groups. The effects include both physical and non-physical factors, the

---

[199]Wikipedia, Culture, Section 6, Cultural Studies.

[200]Wikipedia, Culture, Section 5, Sociology; *Macionis, John J; Gerber, Linda Marie (2011). Sociology. Toronto: Pearson Prentice Hall. p. 53. ISBN 9780137001613. OCLC 652430995.*;

material and the non-material, the secular and the spiritual. Sociology is a broader aspect of culture. The sociology of culture concerns culture as manifested in society.

Relationships between popular culture, political control, and social class were early and lasting concerns in the field.[201] The study of culture and sociology are important aspects in understanding one's beliefs or non-beliefs, theism or anti-theism

Sociology and culture are important to consider when addressing the question of spirituality, morals, virtues, and belief systems. They cannot be separated. They coexist and are integrally interconnected.

---

[201]Id.

CHAPTER IV

Impact of Relativism/Humanism/Secularism/Materialism/Scientism On The Religious Worldview

Relativism, humanism, secularism, materialism, and scientism can color a religious viewpoint as much as culture and sociology discussed above. These concepts are also relevant and material in analyzing the impacts on one's thinking and belief systems. Let's define these terms:

Humanism—"A philosophical and ethical stance that emphasizes the value and agency of human beings, individually and collectively, and generally prefers critical thinking and evidence (rationalism and empiricism) over acceptance of dogma or superstition."[202] "A system of thought and reasoning based on human values and interests, often without accepting the beliefs of religion. A belief system based on the principle that people's spiritual and emotional needs can be satisfied without following a god or religion."[203] Humanism is often tied to and integrated with the philosophy of secularism.

---

[202] Wikipedia, Humanism, p 1.

[203] *Cambridge Dictionary*, Humanism, (https//dictionary.cambridge.org/us/dictionary/english/humanism)

Secularism–"Indifference to or rejection or exclusion of religion and religious considerations."[204] "Secularism is the principle of the separation of government institutions and persons mandated to represent the state from religious institution and religious dignitaries (the attainment of such is termed secularity)."[205]

Materialism–"A tendency to consider material possessions and physical comfort as more important than spiritual values."[206] "Materialism is the attitude of someone who attaches a lot of importance to money and wants to possess a lot of material things. ... Materialism is the belief that only physical matter exists, and that there is no spiritual world."[207]

Scientism–"Thought or expression regarded as characteristic of scientists and excessive belief in the power of scientific knowledge and techniques. Scientism is a term generally used to describe the facile application of science in unwarranted situations not amenable to application of the scientific method. In the philosophy of science, the term 'scientism' frequently implies a critique of the more extreme expressions of logical positivism and has been used by social scientists."[208] Scientism is self-refuting philosophy. Propositions cannot be imperically proven or disproven philosophically. God created science as a tool for us to use to prove

---

[204]*Merriam-Webster Dictionary*, Secularism (https://www.merriam-webster.com/dictionary/secularism)

[205]Wikipedia, Secularism, p 1.

[206]*Oxford Dictionary*, Materialism (https://en.oxforddictionaries.com/definition/materialism)

[207]*Collins English Dictionary*, Materialism (https://www.collinsdictionary.com/us/dictionary/english/materialism)

[208]Wikipedia, Scientism, p1.

certain realities of this universe. However, God is not bound to this universe. One cannot find God through scientism.[209]

Relativism—Relativism is the idea that views are relative to differences in perception and consideration. There is no universal, objective truth according to relativism; rather each point of view has its own truth." "Truth relativism" is the doctrine that there are no absolute truths, i.e., that truth is always relative to some particular frame of reference, such as a language or a culture (cultural relativism). "The Catholic Church, especially under Pope John Paul II and Pope Benedict XIV, has identified relativism as one of the most significant problems for faith and morals today."[210]

Relativism is the most dangerous threat to determining the spiritual truth today. It is the theory that there are no absolute truths, but rather all truth is relative. Nothing is absolute. Nothing is the truth, because truth is relative. Nothing is true for everybody. As it applies to morals and ethics, it says that a person cannot impose his or her morality on another. Everyone is free to believe what they want. There is no truth. And because there is no truth, there cannot be wisdom, because wisdom seeks out the truth. Wisdom and spiritual growth become irrelevant.[211] This is a very dangerous philosophy.

Existentialism and Volunteerism—Things are true because I want them to be true. This means that one's existence trumps any other reason or truth. One's freedom determines the truth. Volunteerism means trumping intellect with will. Casey vs. Planned Parenthood, 505 US 833 (1992), adopted this philosophy in upholding the prior

---

[209]Barron, supra.

[210]Google Dictionary, Relativism; Wikipedia, Relativism

[211]Kelly, Matthew, *The Four Signs of a Dynamic Catholic* (DynamicCatholic.com, 2012), 82–86.

decision of Roe vs. Wade, 410 US 113 (1973)—it belongs to the very nature of one's liberty to determine the meaning of everything. These are based on the philosophy of "liberty interests" and "privacy interests." There is no common truth—comes down to individual will and prerogatives, supported by the power of the US Supreme Court, rather than an appeal to objective truth. Nietzsche (1844–1900), German philosopher, refers to this power position as "Übermensch," who by sheer power of will determines his or her own truth. In Nietzsche's world, the Übermensch can replace God. Modern existentialism follows this philosophy. Existence (freedom) proceeds essence (who I am.) Truth is trumped by will. Volunteerism can lead to violence rather than good debate or argument. For example, atheism depends on existentialism. Things are true because one says so. There is no common truth—only a clash of wills. We are now seeing this on the Internet and TV all the time.[212]

It is my opinion that these six "ism's" have done more harm than virtually anything else to deter and distract individuals, including our youth, from the provable truths of God, the Trinity, and Christianity. The philosophical and intellectual shift is trending from a God-centered universe and dependence now to an ego-centrist universe and attitude where the individual has all the answers about the universe and about spirituality as well as their own versions of a "god" or supreme being. There is clearly a growing separation from God and little consideration of an eternal life after death.

Interestingly, in Europe the spiritual situation is even more desperate than here in the US. Perhaps this is a prophecy of where the US is headed. In Europe, Christianity, and Catholicism in particular, is being marginalized by secularism and socialism, in particular, at

---

[212]Barron, supra.

an ever-increasing rate. Church attendance in many countries is half of what we describe as a crisis here in the US. Germany has 12% Sunday Mass attendance. Italy is at 11%. France at 4%. And the Scandinavian countries are at about 1%. In Australia, secularism is taking its toll on Catholics. Many are bored, tired, fed up, or disinterested with all things spiritual, particularly with organized religion, and especially the Catholic Church.[213]

---

[213]Kelly, Matthew, *The Four Signs of a Dynamic Catholic* (Beacon Publishing, 2012), 192-3.

CHAPTER V

Recent Polls and Surveys On Reasons For Youth Leaving The Christian Faith

A recent 2018 Pew Research Center Report polled a group of American "nones," i.e., a group that answers "nothing in particular" when asked if they identify within a specific religious group. Most are ex-Christians and most are under the age of 35.[214] These groups fall into both the Gen Y (millennials), ages 23–37, and Gen Z (age 22 and younger).

The Pew poll identified five reasons for leaving the Christian faith ("nones") in direct response "agreeing" to carefully formulated Pew questions.

1. Question a lot of religious training (51%),
2. Don't like the positions churches take on social/political issue (46%),
3. Don't like religious organizations (34%),
4. Don't like religious leaders (31%),
5. Religion is irrelevant to me (26%), and

---

[214]Wallace, J. Warner, "Young Christians are Leaving the Church–Here's Why," (www.foxnews.com, September 9, 2018).

6. No longer believe in God [215]

Becky Alper read the same data slightly differently in her article for Pew Research. She found the following stats for "nones":
1. Question religious teachings (60%),
2. Opposition to positions taken by the church on social/political issues (49%),
3. Dislike religious organizations (41%),
4. Don't believe in God (37%),
5. Religion is irrelevant to me (36%), and
6. Dislike religions leaders (34%) [216]

Wallace points out in his article that these survey results are not necessarily definitive. The Pew survey structured the questions and did not allow for individual responses. Most of the surveyed youth indicated that none of the reasons posed in the Pew survey were that important in their decision to abandon their religious identity. Instead, Wallace posits that the "real reasons" for young Christians leaving the faith can be found in a prior 2016 Pew survey, allowing individuals to answer in their own words. In that prior study, the respondents who answered as "nones" indicated they no longer believed in the truth of religion. Many indicated that their views of God had evolved and some said they were going through a "crisis of faith." Specific responses are listed as follows:[217]
1. Learning about evolution when I went to college,
2. Religion is the opiate of the people,
3. Rational thought makes religion out the window,
4. Lack of any sort of scientific or specific evidence of the creator,

---

[215] Id.

[216] Alper, Becky, "Why America's 'nones' Don't Identify with a Religion," Pew Research Center (www.pewreserch.org, August, 8, 2018).

[217] Id.

5. I just realized somewhere along the line that I didn't really believe it,
6. I'm doing a lot more learning, studying and kind of making decisions myself rather than listening to someone else,
7. Some believed in God but in their own way, and
8. Some were seeking "enlightenment" and were open minded [218]

Pew Research in 2015 also found that some of the reasons for falling away to be:
1. Lack of belief,
2. Science,
3. Common sense, logic or lack of evidence,
4. Don't like hierarchical nature of religious groups,
5. Religion too much like business, and
6. Clergy sex abuse scandals[219]

A Christian group conducted a survey in 2016 and found the following reasons for leaving the church:
1. Because I grew up and I realized it was a story like Santa or the Easter Bunny,
2. As I learn more about the world around me and understand things that I once did not, I find that the thought of an all-powerful being to be less and less believable,
3. Catholic beliefs aren't based on fact. Everything is hearsay from back before anything could be documented, so nothing can be disproved, but it certainly shouldn't be taken seriously,
4. I realized that religion is in complete contradiction with the rational and scientific world, and to continue to subscribe to a religion would be hypocritical,

---

[218] Id; Pew Research Center, "Choosing a New Church or House of Worship" (2015).

[219] Id.

5. Need proof of something, and
6. It no longer fits into what I understand of the universe[220]

It is Wallace's view that the essence of the 2016 and 2018 survey responses is a declining belief in the existence of God. He opines that when someone walks away from the faith, it is usually the result of intellectual skepticism. Ex-Christians will inevitably describe religious beliefs as innately blind or unreasonable.[221] Ex-Christians often leave the Church because they don't think anyone in the Church can answer their questions or make the case for Christ, Christianity, or God.

However, these statements do not reflect a knowledge or understanding of the rich and complete body of strong scriptural, philosophical, and historical evidence proving beyond any reasonable doubt the true and real existence of God, the Father and Creator, God the Son, Jesus Christ, Savior, and God the Holy Spirit (consubstantial as the Holy Trinity), the truth of Christianity as the only true religion and the Christian Church, the only true Church, founded by Jesus, and finally the opportunity for salvation and eternal life with the Holy Trinity in Heaven![222] For a person to make an enlightened, intelligent decision on the supernatural, one must consider the possibility of a divine and eternal God who loves each of us and wants the best for us as His children.

I make that case on each of these key points of belief, in my second book, *Christianity on Trial: A Case for Christ*. In that book, I carefully lay out the scriptural and scientific evidence, historicity, historical direct and circumstantial evidence, expert and lay witness opinion introduced into a hypothetical federal court

---

[220] Id; Gray, Mark M, CARA National Study, (Center for Applied Research in the Apostolate, 2016).

[221] Id.

[222] Id.

proceeding by documentary evidence and oral testimonial evidence, all of which are competent, material, relevant, and wholly credible. After reading that book, I believe you would agree with me there is no rational or logical reason to deny your God or the Christian faith. I incorporate summaries of that evidence below in proving the existence of God. There are also many other authors who have written similar "proof" books on various aspects of Christianity. I commend all of them to your reading on the issue of authenticity and credibility of the Christian Church being the only one and true church established over history.

As Wallace points out in his article, look to Psalm 19:1, which discusses the fine-tuning of the universe, and John 10:38 and 16:8, which reflect on the indirect and direct evidence of God through Jesus' miracles. The disciples were eyewitnesses to many of Jesus' teachings and miracles helping those in need, as mentioned in Acts 4:33.[223]

If you are a non-believer, "none," or a marginal Christian with doubts, I suggest it is time for you to take the challenge and time to explore the case for Christ and Christianity more thoroughly. The clear evidence is there!

Apparently, many youth feel they are being ignored and no one has sought them out or reached out to them with credible replies to their concerns. For that very reason, I step up with this book and do my best to address each of the responders' comments above in the following chapters, giving a fair Christian response.

Meanwhile, let's continue to explore some other commentaries on the topic.

J. Wallace has also written extensively elsewhere on this trend of youth leaving the faith. He recently updated a previous article,

---

[223]Id.

"Are Young People Really Leaving Christianity?"[224] In this article, he summarized much research from other authors as follows:

Spiritual Life of Teenagers

The majority of US teenagers are incredibly inarticulate about their faith, religious beliefs and practices, and its place in their lives. Many grow up on homes where parents did not live an active faith, were not devoted to a regular practice of the faith including attending Sunday services, reading the bible with the family, open prayer life in the home; repentance; clear devotion to God, and passing on the Christian faith to their children. Parents care for the physical and educational health of their children. However, more and more, parents are abandoning their children's spiritual health. Instead, children have been left prey to the attractions of the physical world. That is where they find solace, acceptance, and happiness. They have minimalized the presence and importance of God in their lives. They are "going it alone" or in cadence with their peers. They are placing less and less trust in God to help them through this life. And their moral standard and compass is moving from the spiritual and holy to the secular and unholy.

Teenagers are calling their new lifestyle "Moralistic Therapeutic Deism," which refers to a God who exists, created and orders this world, and watches over humans on earth. This God wants people to love Him and to be morally good, loving and fair to each other as taught in the Christian Bible and by other religions. The central goal in life is to be happy, fulfilled, and to feel good about oneself. God is not involved in day-to-day lives, except when He is needed and asked to resolve a problem. Good people go to

---

[224]Wallace, J Warner, UPDATED: "Are Young People Really leaving Christianity?" (www.coldcasechristianity.com, January 29, 2018).

Heaven.[225] Societal philosophical secularism and materialism are winning out over Christian spirituality and holiness in this live. The consequences of this "battle of the principalities" will be eternal for each of us in the life hereafter.

This begs the question: What happens to these youth as they move into adulthood and the business world. Where do they find their hope, trust, direction, and perseverance? The political world is often in a state of turmoil and deadlock. Nothing gets done, just continued bickering and stonewalling for political advantage. Where is the professional example for our youth? The business world is often caught up in blistering one-upmanship sometimes with the mentality of "anything goes" in business, as long as you win. The ends justify the means! Where is the professional and moral compass there? Where are the righteous examples for our merging youth to follow that will lead to a happy and fulfilling life? And, more importantly, are they prepared spiritually for the eternal life hereafter?

Religious training at home is critical to helping a youth experience a balanced life with the ability to properly judge the secular and the spiritual. A well-known proverb says, "Train a child in the way he should go, and when he is old he will not turn from it" (Proverbs 22:6). Another scriptural passage reminds parents to teach their children God's commands: "Impress (God's commandments) on your children. Talk about them when you sit at home and when you walk along the road ..." (Deuteronomy 6:4–9). Scripture is clear—parents play a critical role in the proper upbringing of their children. They should not forget to properly balance their children's physical health, mental health and education, and spiritual health, just like a three-legged stool. Without any one of the legs, the stool falls.

---

[225]Id; Smith, Christian and Melinda Lundquist Denton, *Soul Searching: The Religious and Spiritual Lives of American Teenagers* (Oxford Press, 2005).

Sadly, young people between the ages of 18–34 consistently hold to heretical views in their personal theologies, in greater percentages than older respondents.[226]

Attitude of College Professors

72% of college faculty members describe themselves as politically liberal, based on 1999 research of the North American Academic Study Survey (NAASS), up from 39% in a similar 1984 survey by the Carnegie Foundation for the Advancement of Teaching.[227] About 25% are professing atheists or agnostics (compared to 5–7% of the American public). Only 6% say the Bible is the "actual word of God." 75% say religion does not belong in public schools.[228] Faculty who are secular/liberal are more likely to favor separation of religion and government, and those who are religious and conservative are more likely to advocate a closer connection between religion and government.[229]

Decreasing Christian Population in General

The number of people who identify themselves as Christian has dropped from 85% in 1990 to 78% in 2008 to 70.6% in 2014. About 52% of American adults identify themselves as Protestant or other non-Catholic Christian denominations. That's down from

---

[226] Id; Ligonier Ministries and Lifeway Research (2015).

[227] Id; Rothman, Stanley and S. Robert Lichter, Neil Nevitte, "Politics and Professional Advancement Among College Faculty" (2005).

[228] Id; Gross, Neil and Solon Simmons, "How Religious are America's College and University Professors?" (2006).

[229] Id; The Institute for Jewish and Community Research Review–Staff, "The Religious Beliefs and Behavior of College Faculty" (2007).

60% in 1990. Catholics have declined from 23% to 20%.[230] The trend is away from formal religious affiliation. Today, approximately 21% of Americans say they are either atheist, agnostic, or have no religious affiliation. This is up 6% since 2008. Americans are saying religion is losing its influence on American life.[231] The millennial segment of our population claims to be about 40% "nones" as noted above. On the other hand, 40% of Americans say they have strong religious affiliations. The number of those who are not strongly affiliated but are leaving the church is down from 55% in 1990 to 42% in 2015. Those claiming no affiliation with religion have grown from 8% to approximately 22% of the population during the same time.[232] Only 8% attend church multiple times in a week. Those who attend "sometimes" have dropped from 79% to 69% from 1990 to 2015. Those who never attend have risen from 14% to 25% in the same time frame. Only 33% describe the Bible as the "literal Word of God." Those holding the Bible is "inspired" have dropped from 53% to 47% from 1990 to 2015. Those claiming the Bible is a "book of fables" have risen from 15% to 21% during the same time.

In a 2002 study by the Gallup Poll, they found that teens are more religious during their early teen years, and it begins to decline near adulthood. When asked about the importance of religious beliefs, 63% of 13–15 year-olds answered "very important" compared to 52% of 16–17 year olds. Church attendance also drops during the teen and young adult years and begins to climb as adults age. 54% of teens aged 13–15 reported attending church in the last week, as did 15–16% of the 16–17 year-olds. This figure drops to 32% among 18–29 year-olds but rises to 44% among 50–64 year

---

[230] Id; Pew Research Center, "America's Changing Religious Landscape" (2015).

[231] Id; Gallup National Poll, "Five Key Findings on Religion in the U.S." (2016).

[232] Id, Sociological Science Study, "The Persistent and Exceptional Intensity of American Religion: a Response to Recent Research" (2017).

olds and up to 60% for those 75 and older. As for claiming church or synagogue membership, the numbers are 59% of 16–17 year-olds, 60% of 18–29 year-olds, 72% of 50–64 year-olds and 80% of those aged 75 and older.[233]

Among teen Christians, 63% don't believe that Jesus is the Son of the one and only true God, 51% don't believe Jesus rose from the dead, and 68% don't believe that the Holy Spirit is a real entity. Only 33% say that church will play a part in their lives when they leave home.[234] At least 50–67% of young people will step away from the Christian faith while attending a non-Christian college or university.[235] Another study tells us that 70% will leave the faith in college, and only 35% will return. College and universities and the workforce are strong reasons for young people to leave church.[236] A relatively recent study indicates that emerging adults are significantly less religious: only 15% embrace a strong religious faith, 30% tend to customize their faith to fit the rest of their lives, 15% believe in some higher power but are not sure what it means, 25% may claim to be religious—but it doesn't matter—5% said they had little or non-exposure to religious people, ideas, or organizations, and 10% are skeptical of religion and reject the idea of personal faith—they are critical, derogatory, and antagonistic toward religion.[237] An interesting study assessed some of the reasons for the increasing disinterest in religion. They concluded from their studies that young adults are unable to think coherently

---

[233] Id; Gallop Poll Study, "The Religiosity Cycle" (2002).

[234] Id; McDowell, Josh and David H, Bellis, *The Last Christian Generation* (Green Key Books, 2006).

[235] Id; Kingsriter, Dalyton A., "Assemblies of God Study" (2007).

[236] Id; "Lifeway Research Study," Lifeway Research and Ministry development (2007)

[237] Id; Smith, Christian and Patricia Snell, "Souls in Transition: The Religious and Spiritual Lives of Emerging Adults" (2009).

about moral beliefs and problems. They have an excessive focus on consumption and materialism as the good life. The prevalent lifestyle is inclined toward drinking, drugs, and sex.[238] As always, one must carefully assess these conclusions for accuracy. However, the message, at least, is that there are trends in this direction. The undeniable conclusion I take from these reports is that religion and spirituality are taking a back seat to secularism, materialism, humanism, scientism, and relativism! This is a very disturbing and dangerous trend.

A very recent study summarizes quite well the findings over the last few decades: 39% of teens and young adults (aged 18–29) are religiously unaffiliated—three times the unaffiliated rate for seniors (65 and older). Young adults are four times more likely than their peers a generation ago (Gen X) to identify as religiously unaffiliated. In 1986 only 10% of young adults claimed no religious affiliation. In the 1970s only about 34% of Americans were raised in religiously unaffiliated homes. By the 1990s 53% were unaffiliated households. Today over 66% of households are unaffiliated. And these individuals tend to remain unaffiliated throughout life. [239]

Polls of proclaimed atheists found some common characteristics among "determinedly irreligious" college students:
1. They had attended Church at one time,
2. The mission and message of their churches was vague,
3. They felt their churches offered superficial answers to life's difficult questions,
4. They expressed their respect for those ministers who took the Bible seriously,

---

[238] Id; Smith, Christian, Kari Christoffersen, Hillary Davidson, Patricial Snell Herzogg, *Lost in Transition: The Dark Side of Emerging Adulthood* (Oxford University Press, 2011).

[239] Id; Cooper, Betsy, Daniel Cox, Rachel Lienesch, Robert P Jones, *Exodus: Why Americans are Leaving Religion – and Why They're unlikely to Come Back* (2016).

5. Ages 14–17 were decisive periods,
6. The decision to embrace unbelief was often an emotional one, and
7. The Internet factored heavily into their conversion to atheism.[240]

Pew Research in 2015 found, as noted above, that some of the reasons given for falling away are:
1. Lack of belief,
2. Science,
3. Common sense, logic, or lack of evidence,
4. Don't like hierarchical nature of religious groups,
5. Religion too much like business, and
6. Clergy sex abuse scandals.

Finally, polls of Gen Z specifically found the following for the younger age group:[241]

59% identify as Christian or Catholic (down from 75% for "elders"), 21% say they are atheist or agnostic (up from 11% for "elders"), and 14% say they have no religious affiliation (up from 9% for "elders"). The reasons given include:

1. I have a hard time believing that a good God would allow so much evil or suffering in the world (29%),
2. Christians are hypocrites (23%),
3. I believe science refutes too much of the Bible (20%),
4. There are too many injustices in the history of Christianity (15%),
5. I used to go to church, but it is not important to me anymore (12%), and

---

[240] Id; Taunton, Larry, *Listening to Young Atheists: Lessons for a Stronger Christianity* (Fixed Point Foundation, 2013).

[241] Id; Barna Research Group, Gen Z: "The Culture, Beliefs and Motivations Shaping the Next Generation" (2018).

6. I had a bad experience at church with a Christian (6%).

Students in this age group struggle to reconcile science with the Bible: 24% side with science (up from 16% with Gen X), 31% believe science and the Bible refer to different aspects of reality (up from 25% with Gen X), 28% believe science and the Bible can be used to support each other (down from 45% with Gen X), and 17% consider themselves on the other side of the Bible (up from 13% with Gen X but down from 19% with the millennials [Gen Y]).

Interestingly, Gen Z holds positive perceptions of the Church:
1. The church is a place to find answers to live a meaningful life (82%),
2. The church is relevant for my life (82%),
3. I feel like I can "be myself" at church (77%), and
4. The people at church are tolerant of those with different beliefs (63%).

However, Gen Z also holds negative feelings about the Church:
1. The church seems to reject much of what science tells us about the world (49%),
2. The church is overprotective of teenagers (38%),
3. The people at church are hypocritical (36%),
4. The church is not a safe place to express doubts (27%),
5. The faith and teaching I encounter at church seem rather shallow (24%), and
6. The church seems too much like an exclusive club (17%).

On the question of whether the church is important to them, they received the following responses:
1. The church is not relevant to me (59%),
2. I find God elsewhere (48%),
3. I can teach myself what I need to know (28%),

4. I think the church is out of date (20%),
5. I don't like the people who are in the church (15%), and
6. The rituals of church are empty (12%).

Reaching Out to the Gen Y Millennials and Gen Z

Some suggestions for stopping and reversing some of these troubling trends of our youth leaving the church include better engagement at home and from the church. Parents and clergy need to reach out to the youth in a meaningful and non-condescending manner to interest them in the church again, and to show them how the church is truly relevant to their lives and that all of the spiritual propositions that matter can be absolutely proven.

Family

One book addresses a 35-year study of families, focusing on how religion is passed across generations and the importance of embracing religion in the family:
1. Parents continue to be the single greatest influence on their children's faith;
2. When a child sees and hears that faith actually makes a difference in mom and dad's lives, they are much more likely to follow suit;
3. Young adults are more likely to share their parents' religious beliefs and participation if they feel that they have a close relationship with those parents; and
4. Young Christians who leave the faith are far more likely to return when parents have been patient and supportive—and

perhaps more tolerant and open than they had been before the prodigal's departure.[242]

Church

Ways to keep millennials connected to the Church:
1. Develop meaningful relationships with millennials;
2. Teach millennials to study and discern what's happening in the culture;
3. Help millennials discover their own mission in the world, rather than ask them to wait their turn;
4. Teach millennials a more potent theology of vocation or calling; and
5. Help millennials develop a lasting faith by facilitating a deeper sense of intimacy with God.

So this is the research data reflecting some reasons for the troubling trend of our youth moving away from the Church. We can address these causes and stated reasons with care and caution, humility, and sincerity of heart to parents, teachers and the youth themselves. We cannot and must not lecture. We cannot look down our nose at what seems so obvious to us as elders. We cannot condescend. These approaches are anti-biblical. Jesus would not teach in this manner. Instead, we must approach our wonderful and intelligent youth with love, with care and compassion, with understanding, with humility, kindness, bearing the truth with a desire to help them through the questioning of their faith. After all, remember that God gave the youth minds to reason and rationalize. The youth are merely using the tools that God gave them.

---

[242]Id; Bengton, Vern L, Norella M. Putney, Susan Harris (Oxford University Press, 2013)

Summary:

As noted, researchers call responders to religious surveys who claim no particular religious affiliation "nones" as they usually respond "none" on those surveys. Another term of art for them is "unaffiliated."[243] Nones have become a major subject in the evangelization circles. That is the new dedicated focal point for evangelists. This is because the numbers are alarming–see the numbers above. In general, 25% of all US "Christians" are "nones" and millennial "nones" number 40%. The number of Catholic Christian millennial "nones" hits a staggering high of 50%! Overall these groups amount to over 15 million people! Stated another way, for every person entering the church there are six leaving. By comparison, Gen X "nones" number about 15%. Christian churches see this as a very serious problem.[244] The negative trend in Christian spirituality is on a rapid decline. This is alarming to the Church.

There is no one cause. Typically, however, it is due to backsliding over time. Many simply don't agree with the Church on current relevant social matters. Some have had bad personal experiences in the church. Some are disaffected because of the current sex abuse crisis in the Catholic Church. Some don't get any special message at mass. Some find that it is not a friendly or joyful place. And once one leaves the church, one often finds reasons to stay away.[245]

Some of the stated reasons are discussed in the next chapter. They include lack of intellectual belief in God, meaning we are not explaining the faith, and the sustainable central core claims and doctrines of the Catholic Church. Nor are we adequately

---

[243]Barron, Bishop Robert, "Evangelizing the Unaffiliated, Word on Fire Institute Digital Summit," (Word on Fire Institute https://wordonfire.institute/summit2019-recordings, February 18–21, 2019).

[244]Id.

[245]Barron, supra at Stephan Bullivant, "Catholic Disaffiliation."

addressing the sex scandals and other negative perceptions of the church.

Atheists employ relativism to justify their lack of belief–"I'm OK, and I can believe whatever I want." And creation is contingent, caused by things other than a god. Unfortunately, they don't look far enough backward to creation–singularity and the Big Bang. Agnostic deism based on early teachings places their chosen god into everything around us. Nature and god become inseparable. They are not current in their thinking. The greatest challenges facing the Church are self-induced relativism, individualism, and self-invention.[246]

Secularism also plays a major role in the decline of spirituality. Secularism is the principle of separation of the state from religious institutions.[247] The primary weighted focus for many youth has shifted from the spiritual to the material as noted in previous chapters. God is now competing with Amazon and Facebook for attention! As a result, God becomes less relevant in one's day-to-day living. Eternity takes back stage to the temporal life front stage!

One of the ways to start reversing this decline in spirituality is to evangelize on, beauty, goodness and truth. These are objective common denominators recognized by marginal Christians, unaffiliated and "nones" in everyday living. Beauty leads the way, because everyone can agree on what is beautiful in life subject of our five senses. Beauty is really based in the love of God and his goodness reflected through nature and other humans. God's goodness and truth will follow logically in the discussion. Everyone is looking for the truth, goodness, and beauty in their lives. We must move the nones' hearts from subjective truth to objective truth based on God. Of course, God is the source of

---

[246]Baron, at Robert Baron, "Evangelizing the Unaffiliated."

[247]Google Dictionary, "Secularism."

all these desires and earthly manifestations. They all lead back to a good and loving God the Father and creator. It is also very important for the person evangelizing to know their stuff. They must be well versed in scripture and teachings of the Christian church and ready to defend these teachings through apologetics (1 Peter 3:15). We can evangelize "nones" also through philosophical arguments—faith and reason are compatible concepts. God gave us minds to reason toward the ultimate truth of a God. Ultimately, many seek out happiness as the primary goal in their lives. Focused correctly, happiness can lead to internal joy. Joy emanates from love, i.e., serving and doing good things for God and for neighbor. (See Jesus' Great Commandment—Love God with all our heart mind soul and strength and love your neighbor as yourself, Mark 12:30–31).[248]

Scientism is also a significant culprit in the diversion of Catholic Christians from their church. Scientism is the excessive belief in the power of scientific knowledge and techniques.[249] However, we know the science does not hold all the answers. Science does not answer questions about purpose and meaning of life. God knows everything about you. You are accountable for your sins. Instead, science is the study of the handiwork of God. Science and faith are compatible and work together. Catholics are pro-science. However, spirituality overarches science.[250]

Now the Church has a chance to embrace the gift of our young ones and gently evangelize, teach, and discuss the Christian faith. But we must do it intelligently. We must meet the youth where they are and address the truth to them. We must be able to explain

---

[248]Baron, supra, Chis Kaczor, "Myths of the Catholic Church."

[249]Google Dictionary, "Scientism."

[250]Baron, supra at Stacy Trasancos, "Science and Evangelism."

the story of salvation and address questions through apologetics and love. They will be grateful. Jesus will be grateful.

CHAPTER VI

Christian Responses to Reasons for Leaving The Christain Faith

Let's now address the key reasons young Christians are leaving the Church. I took the liberty to reassemble many of the questions into common groupings of related questions from the many surveys to simplify the responses. Many of the respondents were saying the same thing but in different jargon. Hopefully this will help us "stay out of the weeds" and focus on coalesced key points raised.

Here is my aggregation and restatement of the key issues and reasons raised. Hopefully you will agree on the arrangement:
1. Question much of religious teaching and I just don't believe in God
2. There is no scientific or other evidence of God
3. Science, common sense, and reason give me all the answers and are incompatible with religion and I can learn all I need to know about God and creation on my own without religion
4. I don't like formalized and hierarchical religion and religious leaders
5. Religion is not relevant to my life

Let's address each of these declared reasons in order:

1. Question much of religious teaching and I just don't believe in God

God gives each of us the capacity to understand and believe in Him. (Rom 12:3). Everyone is given the opportunity, but not everyone accepts that free gift. However, whether one accepts or not does not alter the objective reality for everyone else. Reality is reality. True reality is objective. Reality is not subjective. The physical universe is real. We humans are real. Eternity is real. God is real. Yet not everyone believes in God as master designer and creator of everything we can see or sense, as well as everything we cannot.

Why do some reject the notion of a supernatural supreme being and creator? Is it because no one can see God in the physical sense? The bottom line is that many of the younger Y generation and some Zs are moving away from a belief in God, and therefore this discussion. Why are some young Christians rejecting the notion of Jesus Christ as the only begotten Son of God the Father, and our Savior, opening the door for us to join them in Heaven after this earthly life? Why do some reject the concept of the Holy Spirit, the manifestation of Jesus on earth after Jesus' death and resurrection and ascension back into Heaven? Why do younger generations deny the theological concept of the Trinity, which is the Father, Son, and Holy Spirit, three individual divine personalities but consubstantial—acting in unison with the same purpose, primarily for our salvation and the opportunity for us to join them in Heaven? I firmly believe much of this movement is due to a lack of discussion, argument, study and reflection, apologetics, contemplation, and internal thoughtful discernment. Most of us are extremely busy with family, business, and jobs—making a living, surviving, and thriving. We are all caught up in the physical reality of this existence. Little time is left to contemplate the spiritual side of our lives. I would challenge our youth to take the time and consider the spiritual life. This physical existence is short term—up to say 80–90 earth years for most of us. The spiritual life following our temporal earthly life is for eternity. When we put the physical and spiritual on a scale, the later becomes immensely more important than the former. Let's further explore this notion using reason and logic.

When people say they don't believe in God, that statement could have three different connotations. First, God the Father alone. In this context the person could mean they don't believe in God the creator of the universe. Instead they believe in no god at all (atheist) or some god (agnostic) or another god (polytheistic or monotheistic). They just don't believe in the usual monotheistic Christian concept of God. Second, God, in the more inclusive Christian sense, meaning they don't believe in a Christian God the Father and Creator of the universe and God the Son, both human and divine, our Savior who sacrificed Himself by dying for us on the cross to reconcile us back to God the Father because of our sinful nature. Third, some may include The Holy Spirit in their own definition of God, meaning they have rejected the full Trinity.

Because of the different prevailing concepts of "God," I felt it best to address each of the three persons of the Holy Trinity individually, giving the Christian apologetic response and establishing the case for each Person. Hopefully you find the discussion stimulating and meaningful as you ponder your personal take on "God

To properly consider the following discussion, I believe it helpful to reflect on one's faith through introspection. What do I really believe in? What do I have faith in? What is my bias? Once we are honest with ourselves about our "faith" we can proceed to consider the evidence and arguments above. It is important, if one is a marginal believer or nonbeliever to try to leave one's mind open at least to the discussion. After all the evidence is presented and considered, then one can move on to drawing conclusions. ." After you have considered all the evidence below, hopefully, you will share your new insights with the youth within your circle of family of friends.

Faith—What role does faith play?[251] "Faith is confidence or trust in a particular system of religious belief."[252] It is believing without perceivable evidence, based on trusting what cannot be seen but is reasoned:
a. **Scientific Faith**—based on trust in hard physical evidence or evidence calculated by deduction.
b. **Spiritual Faith**—based on trust in God; no earthly source.[253] "Now faith is the substance of things hoped for; the evidence of things not seen" (Heb 11:1).

The word translated as "faith" in the New Testament is the Greek word "πίστις" which can also be translated "belief", "faithfulness", and "trust." There are various views in Christianity regarding the nature of faith. Some see faith as being persuaded or convinced that something is true. In this view, a person believes something when they are presented with adequate evidence that it is true. Theologian Greg Boyd argues to the contrary, that faith includes doubt.

Then there are numerous views regarding the results of faith. Some believe that true faith results in good works, while others believe that while faith in Jesus brings eternal life, it does not necessarily result in good works.

Regardless of which approach to faith a Christian takes, all agree that the Christian faith is aligned with the ideals and the example of the life of Jesus. The Christian sees the mystery of God

---

[251]Horn, Trent, *Why We're Catholic* (Catholic Answers Press, 2017), 14–15.

[252]Wikipedia, Faith, 1; "Faith–Define Faith". *Dictionary.com*. Retrieved October 14, 2015.

[253]Horn, supra, at 5.

and His grace and seeks to know and become obedient to God. To a Christian, faith is not static but causes one to learn more of God and to grow; Christian faith has its origin in God. In Christianity, faith causes change as it seeks a greater understanding of God. Faith is not only fideism or simple obedience to a set of rules or statements. Before Christians have faith, they must understand in whom and in what they have faith. Without understanding, there cannot be true faith, and that understanding is built on the foundation of the community of believers, the scriptures and traditions, and on the personal experiences of the believer. In English translations of the New Testament, the word "faith" generally means "to trust, to have confidence, faithfulness, to be reliable, to assure."[254]

Faith is a key ingredient in any religion, as the believer cannot physically see the spiritual being they might call "god." Scholars debate the spectrum, from blind faith to evidence-based faith.[255] A wonderful example of questioning faith is the doubting Thomas who would not believe the testimony of fellow disciples about the resurrection of Jesus Christ from the dead. He is discussed in John 20:24–31. Thomas did not have firsthand hard scientific observable

---

[254] Wikipedia, Faith, at Section 3, Religious Views, Section 3.3, Christianity; "Strong's Greek: 4102. πίστις (pistis)—faith, faithfulness". biblehub.com. Retrieved 14 October 2015; Wilkin, Robert N. (2012). *The Ten Most Misunderstood Words in the Bible*. Corinth, TX: GES. p. 221; Boyd, Gregory A. *The Benefit of the Doubt*. (Grand Rapids: Baker, 2013), 272. ISBN 978-0-8010-1492-5; "(PDF) Jeremy Myers, The Gospel Under Siege: 3 Views on the Relationship Between Faith and Good Works"; Wuerl, By Donald W. *The Teaching of Christ: A Catholic Catechism for Adults, Edition: 5, revised.* (Huntingdon, IN: Our Sunday Visitor Pub. Division, 2004), 238. ISBN 1-59276-094-5. Retrieved 21 April 2009; Migliore, Daniel L. *Faith seeking understanding: an introduction to Christian theology*. (Grand Rapids, Mich: W.B. Eerdmans, 2004), 3-8; Inbody, Tyron. The faith of the Christian church: an introduction to theology. (Grand Rapids, Mich: William B. Eerdmans Pub, 2005), 1–10; Thomas, Robert L.; Editor, (General New American Standard Exhaustive Concordance of the Bible: Nashville, Tenn.: A.J. Holman, 1981), 1674–75. ISBN 0-87981-197-8.

[255] Wikipedia, supra.

evidence of seeing the risen Christ. He doubted. However, when Jesus appeared to him and the other disciples, so Thomas could see with his own eyes, and he inserted his hand into Jesus' side wound, he then became a believer. The apostle John, in writing his gospel, noted that Jesus also performed many other miracles not recorded so that witnesses might believe. The miracles were intended to be scientific and physically observable faith events to those followers who could physically do what Thomas did. Jesus eventually moved many of his followers from physical eye witness based faith believers to spiritual-based faith believers. The gospel is intended to be a written testimony of this special miracle in the presence on John and the other disciples, including Thomas. " ... because you have seen me, you have believed, blessed are those that have not seen, yet believe" (John 20:30–31). This gospel is persuasive text based of John's observations and testimony so that we, his readers, might be encouraged to also believe as spiritual-based believers, even though we have not seen with our own eyes.[256] And, finally, God asks for our faith and belief in Jesus. Our future depends on it."[36] Whoever believes in the Son has eternal life, but whoever rejects the Son will not see life, for God's wrath remains on them" (John 3:36).

New Testament Scripture in the Bible speak to the theology of faith. There are numerous God-inspired passages given to the Apostles of Jesus' time. I lay out some passages on faith here for you to contemplate. The term "faith" can have two connotations depending on context—faith in God and/or faith in Jesus:

"And Jesus said to him, "Go; your faith has made you well." Immediately he regained his sight and {began} following Him on the road" (Mark 10:52).

---

[256] Id.

"And Jesus answered saying to them, "Have faith in God'" (Mark 11:22).

"And He said to them, 'Where is your faith?' They were fearful and amazed, saying to one another, 'Who then is this, that He commands even the winds and the water, and they obey Him?'" (Luke 8:25).

"And the Lord said, 'If you had faith like a mustard seed, you would say to this mulberry tree, 'Be uprooted and be planted in the sea'; and it would obey you" (Luke 17:6).

"And He said to him, 'Stand up and go; your faith has made you well'" (Luke 17:19).

"I tell you that He will bring about justice for them quickly. However, when the Son of Man comes, will He find faith on the earth?" (Luke 18:8)

"And on the basis of faith in His name, {it is} the name of Jesus which has strengthened this man whom you see and know; and the faith which {comes} through Him has given him this perfect health in the presence of you all" (Acts 3:16).

"The word of God kept on spreading; and the number of the disciples continued to increase greatly in Jerusalem, and a great many of the priests were becoming obedient to the faith" (Acts 6:7).

"Strengthening the souls of the disciples, encouraging them to continue in the faith, and {saying,} 'Through many tribulations we must enter the kingdom of God'" (Acts 14:22).

"Because He has fixed a day in which He will judge the world in righteousness through a Man whom He has appointed, having furnished proof to all men by raising Him from the dead" (Acts 17:31).

"To open their eyes so that they may turn from darkness to light and from the dominion of Satan to God, that they may receive forgiveness of sins and an inheritance among those who have been sanctified by faith in Me" (Acts 26:18).

"That is, that I may be encouraged together with you {while} among you, each of us by the other's faith, both yours and mine" (Rom 1:12).

"For in it {the} righteousness of God is revealed from faith to faith; as it is written, 'but the righteous {man} shall live by faith'" (Rom 1:17).

"For we maintain that a man is justified by faith apart from works of the Law" (Rom 3:28).

"For the promise to Abraham or to his descendants that he would be heir of the world was not through the Law, but through the righteousness of faith" (Rom 4:13).

"Therefore, having been justified by faith, we have peace with God through our Lord Jesus Christ" (Rom 5:1).

"So, faith {comes} from hearing, and hearing by the word of Christ" (Rom 10:17).

"And if Christ has not been raised, then our preaching is vain, your faith also is vain" (1 Cor 15:14).

"Be on the alert, stand firm in the faith, act like men, be strong" (1 Cor 16:13).

"For we walk by faith, not by sight" (2 Cor 5:7).

"Nevertheless, knowing that a man is not justified by the works of the Law but through faith in Christ Jesus, even we have believed in Christ Jesus, so that we may be justified by faith in Christ and not by the works of the Law; since by the works of the Law no flesh will be justified" (Gal 2:16).

"I have been crucified with Christ; and it is no longer I who live, but Christ lives in me; and the {life} which I now live in the flesh I live by faith in the Son of God, who loved me and gave Himself up for me" (Gal 2:20).

"Therefore, be sure that it is those who are of faith who are sons of Abraham" (Gal 3:7).

"For you are all sons of God through faith in Christ Jesus" (Gal 3:26).

"For by grace you have been saved through faith; and that not of yourselves, {it is} the gift of God" (Eph 2:8).

"So that Christ may dwell in your hearts through faith; {and} that you, being rooted and grounded in love" (Eph 3:17).

"And may be found in Him, not having a righteousness of my own derived from {the} Law, but that which is through faith in Christ, the righteousness which {comes} from God on the basis of faith" (Phil 3:9).

"Now faith is the assurance of {things} hoped for, the conviction of things not seen" (Heb 11:1).

"And without faith it is impossible to please {Him,} for he who comes to God must believe that He is and {that} He is a rewarder of those who seek Him" (Heb 11:6).

"Knowing that the testing of your faith produces endurance" (James 1:3).

"Even so faith, if it has no works, is dead, {being} by itself" (James 2:14).

A number of passages also address belief in God and in Jesus, His Son, our savior:

"And saying, 'The time is fulfilled, and the kingdom of God is at hand; repent and believe in the gospel'" (Mark 1:15).

"And Jesus said to him, 'If You can?' All things are possible to him who believes" (Mark 9:23).

"He who has believed and has been baptized shall be saved; but he who has disbelieved shall be condemned" (Mark 16:16).

"But as many as received Him, to them He gave the right to become children of God, {even} to those who believe in His name" (John 1:12).

"So when He was raised from the dead, His disciples remembered that He said this; and they believed the Scripture and the word which Jesus had spoken" (John 2:22).

"If I told you earthly things and you do not believe, how will you believe if I tell you heavenly things?" (John 3:12).

"For God so loved the world, that He gave His only begotten Son, that whoever believes in Him shall not perish, but have eternal life" (John 3:16).

"He who believes in the Son has eternal life; but he who does not obey the Son will not see life, but the wrath of God abides on him" (John 3:36).

"Truly, truly, I say to you, he who hears My word, and believes Him who sent Me, has eternal life, and does not come into judgment, but has passed out of death into life" (John 5:24).

"For this is the will of My Father, that everyone who beholds the Son and believes in Him will have eternal life, and I Myself will raise him up on the last day" (John 6:40).

"Truly, truly, I say to you, he who believes has eternal life" (John 6:47).

"We have believed and have come to know that You are the Holy One of God" (John 6:69).

"And he said, 'Lord, I believe.' And he worshiped Him" (John 9:38).

"Many believed in Him there" (John 10:42).

"Jesus said to her, 'I am the resurrection and the life; he who believes in Me will live even if he dies, and everyone who lives and believes in Me will never die. Do you believe this?'" (John 11:25–26).

"I have come {as} Light into the world, so that everyone who believes in Me will not remain in darkness" (John 12:46).

"Do not let your heart be troubled; believe in God, believe also in Me" (John 14:1).

"Truly, truly, I say to you, he who believes in Me, the works that I do, he will do also; and greater {works} than these he will do; because I go to the Father" (John 14:12).

"Now I have told you before it happens, so that when it happens, you may believe" (John 14:29).

"For the Father Himself loves you, because you have loved Me and have believed that I came forth from the Father" (John 16:27).

"And he who has seen has testified, and his testimony is true; and he knows that he is telling the truth, so that you also may believe" (John 19:35).

"Jesus said to him, 'Because you have seen Me, have you believed? Blessed {are} they who did not see, and {yet} believed'" (John 20:25).

"Paul said, 'John baptized with the baptism of repentance, telling the people to believe in Him who was coming after him, that is, in Jesus'" (Acts 19:4).

"This is His commandment, that we believe in the name of His Son Jesus Christ, and love one another, just as He commanded us" (1 John 3:23).

"We have come to know and have believed the love which God has for us. God is love, and the one who abides in love abides in God, and God abides in him" (1 John 4:16).

"These things I have written to you who believe in the name of the Son of God, so that you may know that you have eternal life" (I John 5:13).

Faith is much more than believing God exists. It also includes a personal relationship with Him. We sense His love in His creation. He is real and interacts continually with us. Atheists/agnostics do not believe this—they accept nothing beyond their physical senses in the observable universe; deists believe that the universe and God both exist and are one, but there is no interaction; theists believe that both the universe and God exist and that God interacts with his creation, including each of us. Atheists/agnostics have no faith, deists see faith as futile. Only Christian theists believe faith works to interconnect us with our God (Father, Son and Holy Spirit) and that He responds to prayers. This is called taking a "leap of faith."[257] I discuss this concept in greater detail below.

Now with an understanding of faith, from all perspectives, let us move into the evidentiary proofs corroborating the existence of and justifying belief and faith in God the Father, Jesus the Son, and the Holy Spirit.

God the Father, Creator

Philosophical proof—Philosophy is the study of general and fundamental problems concerning matters such as existence, knowledge, values, reason, mind and language. In Classical antiquity, philosophy is generally divided out into natural philosophy, i.e.,

---

[257]Id, at slide 36.

the study of nature, moral philosophy, i.e., the study of goodness, right and wrong, and metaphysical philosophy, the study of existence, causation, spirituality and God.[258]

Plato and Aristotle had earlier weighed in on this issue using philosophical deductive reasoning. Desire for perfection that can't be satisfied here on earth during our lives infers we were instilled with a supernatural desire and a life after with a perfect God. Plato and Aristotle called these the Five Transcendental Desires—love, perfect justice, beauty, truth, and home.[259] How could these lofty goals/desires have been derived from a mere human? They are mightier than man. They are part of the divine law of God, instilled in each of us. They could be only sourced with a higher supernatural being—God.

Here are the basic philosophical arguments for the existence of God:

1. Uncaused Being. St Thomas Aquinas (1225–1274) reasoned a God:[260]
   1. There must an uncaused (original) being which always existed with nothing before it,
   2. The uncaused being must be unrestricted,
   3. There can be only one uncaused, unrestricted being, and
   4. The unrestricted, uncaused being must be the ultimate cause of everything else that exists.
2. Desire for perfection. It can't be satisfied here on earth during our lives, which shows we were instilled with a supernatural desire and a life after with a perfect God. Plato and Aristotle

---

[258]Wikipedia, Philosophy.

[259]Id, at slides 25–29.

[260]Spitzer, Fr. Robert, Essential 3: Proof of God's Existence, Credible Catholic (Magis Center, www.crediblecatholic.com, 2017) slides 6-20.

called these the Five Transcendental Desires—love, perfect justice, beauty, truth and home.[261]

3. Faith plays a role. As discussed above, faith is much more than believing God exists. It also includes a personal relationship with Him. We sense His love in this creation. He is real and interacts continually with us. Atheists/agnostics do not believe this—they accept nothing beyond their physical senses in the observable universe; deists believe that the universe and God both exist, but there is no interaction; theists believe that both the universe and God exist, and that God interacts with his creation, including each of us. Atheists/agnostics have no faith, deists see faith as futile. Only Christian theists believe faith works to interconnect us with our God, and that He responds to prayers. This is called taking a "leap of faith."[262] I would suggest that some scientists, secularists, and materialists, including many millennials, feel they have the science and physical evidence to prove the nonexistence of God; the lack of need for a God as all their desires are fulfilled here on earth. Therefore, they logically reason from their premises that there is no need for faith, as there is nothing to believe in or, at least, no need to believe in it. The problem with this logic is that it is founded on a false premise. One needs to probe deeper and ask, "How was this universe designed and created? Where did energy and matter come from?" It certainly did not appear spontaneously. There had to be some cause, as St Thomas Aquinas argues. In fact, there is a God—a God who created the universe and each of us, who loves us very much, as amply proven in this chapter. And, there is a need to believe in this God as there is a Heaven and a Hell, and the entire eternal life

---

[261] Id, slides 25-29.

[262] Id, slide 36.

for your soul depends on which choice you make before your body and mind cease to exist.
4. Conscience. If you have ever heard your own conscience advise you that something you plan to do is wrong and ill advised, and in fact and reality it is, you have heard the voice of God. He was speaking to your soul, your spirit. That is a part of your makeup, separate and apart from your body and mind. You can reason the existence of God. But He will take you one step further and prove to you that He exists when He speaks to your spirit. He is your moral compass. He is with you all the time, offering to help you through this life. He created truth, beauty and goodness that surround us every day. He showers you with His graces and wishes for you a full and happy life. And how we answer our conscience and God's help will be judged by Him after death. We all are accountable to our Creator for our actions and words, what we have done and what we have failed to do. God has planted eternity in each of our hearts. God exists at a spiritual level. You have sensed it yourself. In the courtroom we argue *res ipsa loquitor*—the thing speaks for itself. That is a proven fact.

Spiritual and Scientific Proof. Science and theology from the Bible are not in conflict: they both come from the same source—God. Both search for truth. God created science. Both lead to God. God reveals Himself and His truths through scripture, science, and what we observe in our physical world. Science and the Bible are compatible in revealing His truth. The Bible, both OT and NT, inspired by God, gives us the truth to salvation, that we may spend eternity with Him in Heaven. Science corroborates the evidence of truths in the Bible. One might even say that the Bible satisfies the soul, while humanism, scientism, materialism, and secularism satisfy the mind and body. One can indeed find the truth about God when soul mind and body work in unison to that end.

Old Testament—Rules of Nature—"In the beginning God created the heavens and the earth" (Genesis 1:1; NASB). He then created light out of the darkness giving us day and night (day 1), water, sky/heaven, and earth and evening and morning (day 2), dry land/ground separating earth from sea, vegetation, grass and plants (day 3), sun and moon/days and years (day 4), water creatures and birds (day 5), animals, beasts and cattle and man (day 6). God rested on day 7 (Genesis 1:1–31 and 2:1–7; NASB). Please note that Genesis 1–2, suggests neither a material or temporal beginning to the universe. Hebrews 11:3 confirms this by stating: "By faith we understand that the universe was formed at God's command, so that what is seen was not made out of what was visible." God created something out of nothing. These Biblical texts clearly indicate a creation by an Intelligent Designer and Creator. This context is totally in line with the science of the Big Bang Theory of creation discussed in detail below. Once the universe was created, God took time to perfect his creation on earth. Science and theology are totally compatible on the creation of the universe!

Don't get hung up on taking these passages literally. Many scholars contend these dates and the sequence were symbolic and metaphorical, within the limitations of human understanding at the time of the writing of the Book of Genesis. God will not overwhelm us with too much info. He patiently waits until we are ready to absorb and understand. I believe the earth was formed over 4.5 billion years. Radioactive dating confirms scientifically this fact. Radioactive half-life's for certain elements was another creation of God to help advance our understanding of His creation. Again we are peeling back the scientific "onion."

Old Testament Evidence—Scriptural Recording: Abraham, 2,000 BC. The story of near sacrifice of son, Isaac, is authenticated and corroborated as to place (Mount Moriah) and time as described by Moses in the Book of Genesis. Although there is no definitive real evidence confirming his existence, there is good circumstantial evidence. Archaeological finds (Ur to Harran) and his genealogy further corroborate the truth of Abraham's wanderings and settlements. Christian, Muslim, and Jewish scholars all concede Abraham existed.[263]

Scriptural Records—Supernatural Miracles: Moses, 1,450 BC. The story of Passover, plagues, and parting of Red Sea, burning bush, receiving the Ten Commandments from God all described by OT biblical scholars. Mentioned in the Islamic Quran, Jewish Torah, and the Christian OT. The scholarly consensus today appears to be that Moses may have been more legendary than actual.[264] If Moses did exist, as I believe, the account of Moses as described in the Book of Exodus may have been written by him.

Forty-two miracles by God through Moses are reported in the OT (Ex 7:10). 1) Moses' rod turned into a serpent (Ex 4:2–3); 2) The serpent was transformed into a rod (Ex 4:4); 3) Moses' hand was turned leprous (Ex 4:6); 4) Moses' hand was healed of leprosy (Ex 4:7); 5) The rod was turned into a serpent (Ex 4:30); 6) The serpent was turned into a rod (Ex 4:30); 7) Moses' hand was made leprous (Ex 4:30); 8) Moses' hand was healed of leprosy (Ex 4:30); 9) Moses' rod was turned into a serpent (Ex 7:9–10); magicians also did so, (Ex 7:11–12); 10) Moses' rod swallowed the others (Ex 7:12); 11) The Nile River was changed into blood: first plague (Ex 7:14–25; the Egyptian magicians also did so, (Ex 7:22); 12) He created frogs: second plague (Ex 8:1–7); the magicians also did so, (Ex 8:7); 13) He caused the frogs to die (Ex 8:8–15); 14) He converted the dust to lice: third plague (Ex 8:16–19); the magicians could not do this, (Ex 8:18); 15) He created flies: fourth plague (Ex

---

[263]Parrot, Andre, Abraham, Hebrew Patriarch, Encyclopedia Britannica (www.britnnica.com/biography/Abraham); Szulc, Tad, Journey of Faith, National Geographic (www.nationalgeographic.com, December 2001).

[264]Wikipedia, Moses, Historicity.

8:20–24); 16) He made Goshen exempt from flies (Ex 8:22); 17) He removed the flies from Egypt (Ex 8:29–32); 18) The murrain disease was imposed on Egyptian stock: fifth plague (Ex 9:1–7); 19) The stock of Israel was exempt (Ex 9:4–7); 20) He made boils from ashes: sixth plague (Ex 9:8–12); 21) Hail and fire came: seventh plague (Ex 9:13–35); 22) Goshen was exempt from the hail and fire (Ex 9:26); 23) Moses stopped the hail and fire (Ex 9:28–35); 24) Locusts descended: eighth plague (Ex 10:1–15); 25) The locusts were removed (Ex 10:16–20); 26) Darkness came: ninth plague (Ex 10:21–29); 27) Goshen was exempt from the total darkness (Ex 10:23); 28) Death came to Egypt's firstborn: tenth plague (Ex 11–12); 29) Israel's firstborn were exempt from death (Ex 11:7–10); 30) Moses made a path through the Red Sea, congealing the water (Ex 14:21–22); 31) He melted the ice of Red Sea (Ex 14:26–28); 32) The healing waters of Marah (Ex 15:23–26); 33) Bread from heaven (Ex 16:4–35; Num 11); 34) Quail to eat (Ex 16:8–13); 35) Water from the rock (Ex 17:1–7); 36) His victory over Midian (Ex 17:11–13); 37) He quenched the fire of death (Num 11:2); 38) The healing of Miriam (Num 12:13–16); 39) The earth swallowed the rebels (Num 16:28–33); 40) Moses stopped the plague (Num 16:44–50); 41) Water from the rock (Num 20:10–13); 42) The healing of Israel (Num 21:5–9;John 3:14).[265]

If these things did happen as reported in the OT, as I believe, only a superior supernatural force capable of harnessing nature could have caused these miraculous feats. There are historical eye witness reports and now real evidence of chariot parts at the bottom of the Red Sea that provide undeniable proof of

---

[265]https://www.faithfamilybillings.com/.../42-Miracles-and-wonders-done-through-Moses; https://www.google.com/url?sa=t&rct=j&q=&esrc=s&source=web&cd=4&cad=rja&uact=8&ved=2ahUKEwiYvb62u4PhAhWIJjQIHfcRDT0QFjADegQIDBAC&url=https%3A%2F%2Fwww.faithfamilybillings.com%2Fwpcontent%2Fuploads%2F2016%2F08%2F42-Miracles-and-wonders-done-through-Moses.pdf&usg=AOvVaw3K2kTSlhdtYq9mzqu_ThVI.

God's tremendous love for His people—in that case, the Israelites. Archaeological finds corroborate this truth to some degree.[266] Historical evidence shows that the Bible is reliable recordation of history of events and/or circumstantial evidence thereof. The Bible is not mythical. It is historical and, in some instances, allegorical. External observable real and documentary evidence corroborates the Bible and authorship. True historicity!

External Documentary Evidence—OT. Archaeological and Historical evidence—17,000 Ebla Tablets from North Syria (dated at 2,000 BC) discovered in 1975—accurately confirmed a complex system of law and the location of the historical biblical cities of Sodom and Gomorrah, Admah, Zeboiim, and Zoar as cities of the plain (Genesis 13:12). It also proved that Sumerian writing (similar to Hebrew) existed 700 years before Moses, thereby lending credibility to Moses writing Genesis.[267] Ostracon pottery jar inscriptions (2,000 BC) referenced King David; Chariot lynchpins (1,200 BC)—referenced in book of Judges—were chariots used to fight Israelites.[268]

Historical Evidence. Observable evidence supports testimonial evidence proving that the Bible is historical in fact (but not necessarily God inspired) and that it is not mythical. The Bible is both factual and historical, and in some instances allegorical.

Spiritual Evidence—OT, Forward Spiritual Allusions.[269] Scripture is the inspired Word of God. At least 400 references by qualified OT prophets, widely respected in their times as experts in religion

---

[266]Biblical Archaeology Society Staff, "The Exodus: Fact or Fiction, Evidence of Israel's Exodus from Egypt" (Bible History Daily, www.biblicalarchaeology.com, March 28, 2018).

[267]Oborn, Ragnar, "Consider Design, Part 4, Consider the Gospel," (considerthegospel.com, vimeo.com).

[268]Id.

[269]Oborn, supra, "The Opening Case for a Divine Mind in the Biblical Record."

and scripture. 1) Abraham, the most obvious allusion, is that he is about to sacrifice his son on Mount Moriah at God's direction in 2,000 BC. At the time of preparing to sacrifice his son, God redirects him to substitute a ram caught in a nearby thicket. Fast-forward to the construction of Jerusalem on Mount Moriah, and later in 33 AD, the crucifixion of Jesus on behalf of humanity as the sacrificial lamb. The Genesis allusion is inexplicable short of God's direct involvement in both situations. Creative Divine Intelligence was at work here pointing to the location of Jesus' death. 2) Moses – In anticipation of the 10th plague on the Egyptian people (killing of the first born in the Exodus story), God directed the Jews to paint the pillars on their doors with Passover lamb's blood, so that they would be passed over. The blood of the Passover lamb was to be a sign for God's people. Jesus, the lamb of God, suffered and died during the Jewish Passover celebration. Again, Creative Divine Intelligence was at work here also pointing to the time of Jesus' death.[270] The OT was God inspired as were the multiple references to a future Messiah who would die for humanity. Finally, Moses and Elijah appeared to Jesus at the Transfiguration, and Jesus' robes became dazzling white, as witnessed by Apostles Peter, James, and John. Jesus is called "Son" by a voice from the cloud and the Apostle eyewitnesses were admonished to "listen to Him" (Matthew 17:1–8, Mark 9:2–8, Luke 9:28–36). This appearance reported in the Synoptic gospels lends further credibility to the actual existence of Moses in the OT. Further, Peter confirms this eyewitness account in 2 Peter 1:16–18.

---

[270]Oborn, supra, "Reliability of the Bible: Can I Trust the Text?"

Scientific Evidence on Universe—Astronomy and Astrophysics

Big Bang Theory—expanding universe.[271] Planned design was not by chance.[272] Odds of the universe forming without a God-centered organized force is $1/10^{123}$.[273] Prof. Roger Penrose, an atheist and theoretical physicist on space-time and an adherent to the Standard Model Theory on particle physics (discussed below), concludes that the Big Bang was totally unique, and the universe derived from a singular origin—a "singularity." The universe was not a product of a pre-existing steady state condition. Singularity of origin is sometimes called the Big Bang Theory.[274] In fact, the Big Bang theory of an expanding universe was originally contemplated by Belgian Fr. Georges Lemaitre, a Catholic priest. It states that the expanding universe can be traced back to an originating single point. Lemaitre's theory was eventually adopted by Albert Einstein who rearranged his unprovable theorems as a result. It worked, and Einstein was eventually able to prove his General Theory of

---

[271] Trent Horn, *Why We're Catholic*, 17–24; Spitzer, Fr. Robert, Essential 2: Proof of God's Existence, Credible Catholic,(Magis Center, Oborn, Ragnar, "Consider Design, Part 4, Consider the Gospel," (considerthegospel.com, vimeo.com), 2017) slides 12–15; Mario Seiglie, "God and Astronomy, Beyond Today," United Church of God (www.ucg.org, January 23, 2017).

[272] Horn, supra, at 21- 23.

[273] Aczel, Amer, "Why Science Does Not Disprove God," (*Time Magazine*, April 27, 2014) (Based on calculations of British Mathematician Roger Penrose). This is called the Penrose number.

[274] Wikipedia, Big Bang, Section 2.1, Singularity; Roos, M. (2008). "Expansion of the Universe–Standard Big Bang Model". In Engvold, O.; Stabell, R.; Czerny, B.; Lattanzio, J. Astronomy and Astrophysics. Encyclopedia of Life Support Systems. UNESCO. arXiv:0802.2005.

Relativity.[275] Einstein eventually became a theist recognizing that the Big Bang Theory had to have a supernatural source. He did not necessarily believe in the Christian God but he did believe in a supernatural God before he died.

Dr. Tipler, a mathematical physicist from Tulane University writes in his book, *The Physics of Immortality,* that, as a cosmologist for 20 years, he was an atheist. He could not have dreamed that he would subscribe to the Judeo-Christian theology of God. But he did in his book.[276]

Perfect Alignment of Planetary Objects—Consider the odds of a perfect eclipse of the sun by the moon with a slight penumbra. Divide the sun's diameter (864,576 miles) by the moon's (2,159) = 400.52. The distance of the earth from the sun (93,000,000 miles) by the distance of the moon from the earth 239,000 miles) = 389.121.[277] Odds are $1:10^{50}$ that the planets would randomly align perfectly and maintain their orbits.[278]

---

[275]Penrose, Roger, *The Road to Reality*. A Complete Guide to the Laws of the Universe (Vintage, 2004 (later revisions, 2005, 2006, and 2007)); Wikipedia, Road to Reality; Spitzer, Fr Robert, *P1a: Scientific Evidence of God,* Credible Catholic (Magis Center, www.crediblecatholic.com, 2017) slides 13-17; Harris, J. F. *Analytic Philosophy of Religion.*(Springer,2002), *p. 128.* ISBN 978-1-4020-0530-5; Craig, William Lane, *The Ultimate Question of Origins: God and the beginning of the Universe* (Astrophysics and Space Science, 1999), vol. 269, 723–740. doi:10.1007/978-94-011-4114-7_85. ISBN 978-94-010-5801-8; Harris, J. F. *Analytic Philosophy of Religion.* Springer, 2002), 128. ISBN 978-1-4020-0530-5.

[276]Cantoir, Fr. John, Atheism, Hawaii Catholic Herald, (February 9, 2018) p 21; Tipler, Frank, *The Physics of Immortality* (Anchor Books, Random House, 1995), 7, 14.

[277]Metaxas, Eric, "Are Solar Eclipses Proof of God?" (Fox News, August 20, 2017); Asec, "The Solar Eclipse is Against the Odds in ANY Solar System, Evidence to Consider" (December 1, 2012).

[278]Spitzer, Fr. Robert, Essential 2: Proof of God's Existence, Credible Catholic (Magis Center, www.crediblecatholic.com), slide 44.

Physical Constants Gravitational Constant—Fine Tuning. Generally, in physics, a *dimensionless physical constant*, sometimes called a *fundamental physical constant*, is a physical constant that has no units attached and has a numerical value that is independent of the system of units used. Perhaps the best-known example is the fine-structure constant, coupling constant and electromagnetic interaction, α, which has an approximate value of $1/137.036$.[279] The Standard Model of particle physics describes three of the four known fundamental forces (the electromagnetic, weak, and strong interactions, and does not include the gravitational force) in the universe, as well as classifying all known elementary particles.[280] Gravity remains largely unexplained, although scientists believe they have discovered a *graviton*. In speculative theories of quantum gravity, the graviton is a hypothetical elementary particle that mediates the force of gravitation in the framework of quantum field theory (QFT). [281]

Theoretical and experimental particle physicists pursued and continue to explore these matters in the Standard Model—in effect, looking for God's full revelation of the absolute truth of particle physics. However, in the meantime, we do enjoy fairly well-described theories of at least three of the four known fundamental forces. In a sense, God is allowing us to "peel the particle physics onion" to gain deeper understanding into His creation. British cosmologist and astrophysicist Martin John Rees, president of the Royal Society (2005–10) pinpointed six major physical constants enabling the universe and our planet to function. The first two relate to basic forces; the second two fix the size and texture

---

[279]Wikipedia, Dimensionless Physical Constant, 1.

[280]Wikipedia, Standard Model, 1.

[281]Wikipedia, Graviton, 1.

of the universe and determine whether it will live forever; the last two fix the properties of space.[282]

- N, the ratio of the strength of electromagnetism to the strength of gravity for a pair of protons, is approximately 10^{36}. According to Rees, if it were significantly smaller, only a small and short-lived universe could exist.
- Epsilon (ε), a measure of the nuclear efficiency of fusion from hydrogen to helium, is 0.007: when four nucleons fuse into helium, 0.007 (0.7%) of their mass is converted to energy. The value of ε is in part determined by the strength of the strong nuclear force. If ε were 0.006, only hydrogen could exist, and complex chemistry would be impossible. According to Rees, if it were above 0.008, no hydrogen would exist, as all the hydrogen would have been fused shortly after the Big Bang. Other physicists disagree, calculating that substantial hydrogen remains as long as the strong force coupling constant increases by less than about 50%.
- Omega (Ω), commonly known as the density parameter, is the relative importance of gravity and expansion energy in the Universe. It is the ratio of the mass density of the Universe to the "critical density" and is approximately 1. If gravity were too strong compared with dark energy and the initial metric expansion, the universe would have collapsed before life could have evolved. On the other side, if gravity were too weak, no stars would have formed.
- Lambda (Λ), commonly known as the cosmological constant, describes the ratio of the density of dark energy to the critical energy density of the universe, given certain reasonable assumptions such as positing that dark energy density is a constant. In terms of Plank units, and as a natural dimensionless

---

[282]Rees, Martin, *Just Six Numbers: The Deep Forces That Shape the Universe*, Chapter 1: "The Cosmos and the Microworld" (Basic Books, 2000), p. 2.

value, the cosmological constant, Λ, is on the order of 10^{-122}. This is so small that it has no significant effect on cosmic structures that are smaller than a billion light-years across. If the cosmological constant were not extremely small, stars and other astronomical structures would not be able to form.

- Q, the ratio of the gravitational energy required to pull a large galaxy apart to the energy equivalent of its mass, is around 10^{-5}. If it is too small, no stars can form. If it is too large, no stars can survive because the universe is too violent, according to Rees.
- D, the number of spatial dimensions in space-time, is 3. Rees claims that life could not exist if there were 2 or 4 dimensions of space-time nor if any other than 1 time dimension existed in space-time.[283]

In layman's terms, the force that holds an atom's nucleus together is defined as a dimensionless coefficient (epsilon) equal to 0.007. If this value was smaller, say 0.006, only hydrogen atoms would exist in our universe as the force could not hold neutrons and protons together at the nucleus. There could be no life on this planet. The cosmological constant (lambda), noted above, is described by the ratio between the density of the universe's dark energy to the critical density of Planck's energy; it is extremely small. 10^{-122}. If it was different, none of the stars, constellations, galaxies, and planetary systems could have come together.[284] Other constants include entropy (loss of energy and mass) (order

---

[283] Wikipedia, "Fine Tuned Universe, Examples"; Rees, Martin, *Just Six Numbers: The Deep Forces That Shape The Universe*, (New York, NY: Basic Books; First American Edition, May 3, 2001), 4, Lemley, Brad. "Why is There Life?". (Discover Magazine, November, 2000). Retrieved August 23, 2014.

[284] Rucki, Miroslaw, "Tailor-made Universe, Love One Another," Catholic Magazine, No. 34, (AGAPE Publishers, usa@loamagazine.org, 2016), 16–18.

tends to go to disorder), speed of light, and force of gravity.[285] All this is to say the universe and its many constants (typically stated to be upwards of only 25) are held together by both astronomically large and small forces, which are simply beyond any reasonable doubt that they were created and fine-tuned by a Divine Intelligent Creator—God the Father!

Physical Evidence—Earth (Water and Land), Fine Tuning, Geology and Geophysical Sciences. Earth's magma is in constant flux, creating movement of tectonic plates, upheaval of mountains, formation of volcanoes, all perfectly balanced to sustain life and create weather and rain for growing food for human life. Perfectly aligned conditions for life (land, sea, and sky); zone of life—perfect distance from the sun; constant range of temperature from -30 to 120° F; magnetosphere protecting humankind from solar radiation—draws particles to the poles. The size of the earth is perfect. The size and distance of the moon are perfect—do not cause oceans to overrun their shores. The gravitational field holds a thin (50 miles) layer of oxygen and nitrogen in the atmosphere. Earth is the only known planet in our solar system or extraplanetary to hold the right combination of gases to sustain plant, animal, and human life.

Water—water is a colorless, odorless, and tasteless liquid we could not survive without. Our bodies are at least 90% water. Water is a chemically neutral universal solvent.[286] Evaporation distills fresh water from saltwater making it possible for life to be sustained on land.

---

[285]Spitzer, supra, slide 43.

[286]Is There a God? Does God exist" Here are six straight forward reasons to believe that God is really there. EveryStudent.com (www.everystudent.com); The Wonders of God's Creation, Moody Institute of Science (Chicago, IL)

Beauty - the beauty of the earth's environment; just look at multi-colorful brilliance of rainbows, green color of forests and orchards; the multi-faceted color of fuit and vegetables; brilliance of the blue oceans and magnificent sunsets; peaceful natural coexistence and interdependence with other life; joyful life for most everyone; faith, hope and love abound creating joy and happiness; God created all of this because he loves each of us as His creation—Earth is living proof.

Laws of Nature and Physical Constants—Physics, Math, Particle Physics, and Quantum Mechanics (discussed above)—Scientific and Mathematical proof. 1) Laws of math, physics, and science—constants, 2) Mathematics, material world and human consciousness, 3) Mystery of human consciousness, 4) Evolution and faith can coexist, 5) Miraculous inventions of the human mind.[287] Only a supernatural God could design a universe without chaos by employing multiple physical constants to hold it together. God is unerring. He is perfect. He created the math, physics and science to make this happen. Mankind is only beginning to understand the breadth and depth of God's creation. The mass and energy behind the Big Bang from which all scientists agree, came the creation of the universe. God created the stage for the physical universe and all life. Life began through the amalgamation of C, H, O and N on certain planets including the Earth. We are just the right distance from the sun to be in a stable belt of survival for life (the zone of life) as we know it from 4 billion years ago to the present.[288] In Newton's law, it is the proportionality constant connecting the gravitational force between two bodies with the product of

---

[287]Nelson, Robert H, Why God Very Probably Exists: An Economists Five Ways of Thinking Rationally about God, (Mercatornet, June 9, 2017)

[288]Oborn, Ragnar, Consider the Gospel, Part 1 – The Case for God – Considering Design, (Considerthegospel.org, vimeo.com, 2012).

their <u>masses</u> and the <u>inverse square</u> of their <u>distance</u>.[289] The gravitational constant keeps the universe in perfect gravitational balance—the odds are $1:10^{50}$ that this constant could happen randomly, which clearly proves intelligent design, i.e., God![290]

Science and Religion Combined—60% of scientists believe in God![291] Interestingly, this tracks with the number of millennials as described and graphed above at the beginning of this book. The Big Bang, most scientists agree, commenced the existence of the physical universe as we know it. As noted above, Fr. Lemaitre, a Catholic priest and physicist, first defined the Big Bang hypothesis in 1927 and shared it with Albert Einstein, who later proved the continuing expansion of the universe like a balloon from a point source, and eventually his General Theory of Relativity through revised mathematical modeling.[292] This theory has since been corroborated further through advanced telescope/computer verification of the red shift, i.e., celestial objects continue to move apart from each other at greater velocities the further away they are. Gravitational attraction has less influence as the velocity is proportional the distance between objects.. The logical and reasoned argument, from this proven hypothesis, is that something cannot come from nothing. The universe started with an infinitely dense source about 14 billion years ago (earth years), exploded and expanded, and still today, continues to expand with great energy from a single point source. Fr. Robert Spitzer quotes Albert Einstein

---

[289]Wikipedia, Gravitational Constant

[290]Spitzer, Fr Robert, Essential 2: Proof of God's Existence, Credible Catholic (Magis Center, www.crediblecatholic.com, 2017), slide 44.

[291] Id, at slide 11.

[292] Id, at slides 13-40.

as saying, "The more I study science, the more I believe in God."[293] Note that although Einstein may have been a deist, believing in a creator, he did not necessarily believe in the personal Christian God and creator, argued for in this book.

Current-day astrophysicists, as they learn more about the universe, are continuing to prove the correlation between Big Bang cosmology and the existence of God. The evidence is becoming overwhelming. Big Bang atheists, young earth creationist opponents, and skeptic's arguments against intelligent design are being addressed scientifically and theologically.[294] At the time of the Big Bang, "dark matter" was created. It emits no light and exerts a gravitational pull. They may be primordial black holes with great mass.[295] They are cold dark matter, the lack of which is the primary essence of the opponents and skeptic's proof and argument. It has not been physically seen/observed by telescopes. However, it is now being discovered with the help of very powerful telescopes. It is calculated to be 4–5 X the mass of baryonic (ordinary) matter we can see. We can see the inferential impact of gravitational pull on photons and the causative bending of light, just like baryonic matter (protons, electrons, and neutrons) never before experienced.[296] The skeptics are becoming believers!

---

[293] Spitzer, Fr. Robert, "Essential 6: True Happiness, Credible Catholic" (Magis Center, www.crediblecatholic.com, 2017), slide 60.

[294] Ross, Hugh, "Overcoming Objections to the Big Bang Creation Model, Today's New Reason to Believe" (RTB) Blog, (www.reasons.org, February 13, 2017).

[295] Fore, Meredith, Is Dark Matter Made Up of Mini Black Holes from the Big Bang?, Live Science, April 6, 2018.

[296] Ross, Hugh, "More Evidence for God as Dark Matter Confirmation Nears," "Today's New Reasons to Believe (RTB) Blog," (www.reasons.org, January 22, 2018).

Creation of life—DNA. Dr. Antony Flew, a leading spokesperson for atheism for many years, declared in 2004, "Super-intelligence is the only good explanation for the origin of life and the complexity of nature." Prominent in his conclusion were the discoveries of DNA.[297] The reason was that DNA is made up of four chemicals, designated as A, T, G, and C, much like a computer programmed with 1s and 0s. Every cell is made up of a code three billion letters long.[298] It has also been determined that you and I and everyone else share about 99.9% of the same genetic makeup.[299] But no two people are coded exactly alike! What are the odds? Astronomical!

Dr. Francis Collins, director of the Human Genome Project (which mapped the human DNA structure) said that one can "think of DNA as an instructional script, a software program, sitting in the nucleus of the cell."[300]

On June 26, 2000, President Clinton congratulated those who completed the human genome sequencing. President Clinton said, "Today we are learning the language in which God created life. We are gaining ever more awe for the complexity, the beauty, the wonder of God's most divine and sacred gift."[7] Dr. Francis Collins followed Clinton to the podium, stating, "It is humbling for me and awe inspiring to realize that we have caught the first glimpse of our own instruction book, previously known only to God."[301]

Clearly, intelligent design was behind the creation of DNA and its integration into life of all kinds here on planet earth.

---

[297] "Is God Real? Science gives ample reason to believe in God. Why is DNA important?" EveryStudent.com (www.everystudent.com); Healthy-elements.com/atheists.html.

[298] Id; Francis S. Collins, director of the Human Genome Project, *The Language of God,* (Free Press, New York, NY, 2006), 1.

[299] Id; Collins, supra at 125.

[300] Id; Collins, supra at 102.

[301] Id; Francis S. Collins, *The Language of God,* 2 and 3.

According to the Bible, God is not only the author of life our individual existence, but He is the relationship that makes our existence meaningful. All the intangibles in life that we crave... enough strength for any situation, joy, wisdom, and knowing we are loved...God alone gives these to us as we listen to him and trust him. He also is the author of truth, beauty, and goodness. He is our greatest, reliable guide in life. Just as he has engineered DNA to instruct the cell, he offers to instruct us to make our lives function well, for his glory and for our sake, because he loves us.

DNA is another example of clear scientific evidence circumstantially proving God's existence as our Creator and loving Father.

To this point, Paul, the Apostle, perceived and prophesied the eventual revelation of creation:

> Since what may be known about God is plain to them, because God has made it plain to them. For since the creation of the world God's invisible qualities—his eternal power and divine nature—have been clearly seen, being understood from what has been made, so that people are without excuse. (Romans 1:19–21.)

There is no other logical or reasoned explanation for the cause of this phenomenon other than an all-powerful, all-knowing, and purposeful Intelligent Designer—God!

Old Testament Evidence of Historical Truth—Bible—Physical Evidence. Some examples include:

God's miracles are wonders performed by the divine power of God. They were designed to manifest His supernatural glory and also for the benefit of humankind to help their belief in the divine God. They are different from magic and mere human wonders and tricks.[302]

i. Sarah and Abraham bearing a child at very old age (Gen. 17:19; 18:11 and 21:1–8).
ii. He declared the iniquities of the people before the Great Flood (Gen. 6:5–8 and 14) and the destruction of Sodom and Gomorrah (Gen. 19:1–29).
iii. Moses and the burning bush, where God calls Moses to free the Israelites from Egypt (Ex. 3:2 and 10).
iv. He brought plagues to Egypt because Pharaoh refused to allow Moses and his people to leave (Ex. 10:3–20).
v. God parts Red Sea for Moses (Ex. 14:21).
vi. God fed his people for 40 years with mana and quail (Ex. 16:3–36).
vii. God declared he was the God who brought Moses and the people out of bondage (Ex. 20:2).
viii. Moses receives tablets with Ten Commandments from God
ix. God protects Israel from enemies (2 Kings 17:6–23; 19:10–13, 14–20, 25 and 35).
x. He Fed prophet Elijah and widow and son; he stayed with flour and oil for 3½ years (1 Kings 17:16).
xi. He Saved Shadrach, Meshach, and Abed-Nego from the fire (Dan 3:13–20)[303]

---

[302]St Mark Evangelistic Association, Miracles of the Living God, The Awakening, (www.3lotus.com).

[303]Id.

God's Character[304]—Bible and Catholic Christian Tradition:
1. God is One—One God in three equal persons—Trinity—There is no other (Deut 4:39; Isaiah 45:18).[305] God is the one and only Lord God, and there is no other besides Him (Isa 45:5–6). He is unique. There is no one else like Him.
2. God is Spirit. God is not a physical or corporeal being, but rather a spirit. Not visible (John 4:24, Heb 11:27, 1 Tim 1:17). Only the Son has seen Him (John 1:18).
3. God is Holy.[306] God's holiness is transcendent and preeminent. He is morally perfect. God cannot sin and cannot associate with habitual sin or sinners (Psalm 5:4–6). This is counter to his core character and being (Ex. 3:14 and 15:11; Isa. 6:3; Rev 4:8). God tempts no one (James 1:13.) God hates all that is evil (Deut. 25:16).
4. God is Eternal and Immutable.[307] He is without beginning or end. He is the one same and unchanging God forever. He is everlasting. He is the "I am who I am" (Ex. 3:14; Isa 40:28; Rev 1:8). His reign is eternal (Jer. 10:10). God does not change his mind as to His ultimate purpose—our salvation and spending eternity with Him (1 Sam 15:29; Num. 23:19). But He can change his mind, depending on our actions, on how to accomplish that goal (Jer. 19:7–10; Eze. 18:21–24). God is distinct from the universe.[308]

---

[304]Horn, supra, at 25–30.

[305]Washer, Paul David, The One True God (Granted Ministries Press, 3rd Ed, 2007), 12–16.

[306]Washer, supra at 67–72.

[307]Id, 41–45.

[308]RZIM, Beyond Reasonable Doubt, Apologetics Training, (May 1, 2004), p 7.

5. God is Righteous.[309] God acts in ultimate fairness to all in accordance with his nature and character. His works, decrees, and judgments are absolutely perfect (Psalm 7:9, 89:14, and 97:2; Isa. 5:16).
6. God is Faithful.[310] He is worthy of absolute trust, and His people can depend totally on Him with no hesitation. He does everything He promises (Psalm 146:6; 1 Peter 4:19; Isa 14:24; 1 Thess. 5:23–24).
7. God is Love.[311] Love is the essence of God, His very being and nature. Whoever lives in love, lives in God (2 Cor. 13:11; 1 John 4:7–10 and 4:16). God is compassionate, merciful, and kind to each of His children (Psalm 86:5; 2 Cor. 1:3). God is patient (Ex. 34:6; Num. 14:18; 1 Peter 3:20). God is selfless and kind. God loves us. He desires our ultimate good.[312]
8. God is Personal. He feels and acts. He is a spiritual person.[313] We are made in His image.
9. God is Omnipresent.[314] He is everywhere at the same time (Isa. 43:1–2; Mat 18:20).
10. God is Omniscient.[315] God has an intellect. He is all-knowing of the truth yesterday, today and tomorrow—all at the same time; all is instantaneous to Him (Psalms 94:11; Daniel 2:20–22; Job 37:16; Isa. 44:6–8 and 46:9–10; Psalms 139:1–4 and

---

[309] Id, at 79–87.

[310] Id, at 103–111.

[311] Id, at 113–124.

[312] RZIM, supra, 7.

[313] RZIM, supra, 6.

[314] Id, 56–59.

[315] Id, 60–64.

11–12). God is infinitely wise, with a supreme intelligence (Rom. 11:33–36). He knows each of our hearts (1 Kings 8:39).
11. God is Omnipotent.[316] God has a will (Isa 14:27, Eph 1:11). His will is perfect (Romans 12:2). He is all-powerful; created and rules the universe; created the laws that hold the universe together. God is great and more powerful and greater than anything else (Psalms 145:3 and 138:5, CCC 300). He made the heavens and earth (Jer. 32:17; Matt. 19:26). God is creator of all.
12. God is Omnibenevolent. God is love; God is good; God is beauty; God created each of us individually to enjoy all of this with him. His goal is for us to reach heaven and spend eternity with Him. God is relational. It was through the original sin that we lost our relationship with Him (Gen. 3:8–10 and 23–24). We experience death as a result. However, Jesus, God the Son, restored that relationship through his life, death, and resurrection (Luke 19:10, Rom. 5:8–10, Col. 1:19–22).
13. God and Good vs Evil.[317] God can do no evil, and God tempts no one (James 1:13). It is not in His character. God does not create evil; evil is the absence of good; natural evil is a product of His fallen world, which started with Adam and Eve, so it's man's product and not God's; regarding human evil, God does not interfere with our free will; we are free to commit evil; Satan and his demons embody all the spiritual evil. After Satan and his legions of angels were expelled from Heaven by St Michael, no evil exists in heaven—it is a state of perfection; pain and suffering are part of the temporary human condition on earth—love, beauty, and goodness are part of the eternal spiritual condition in Heaven.

---

[316]Id, 53–57.

[317]Horn, supra, 31–33.

Because of the great evil He saw in his creation of man, God allowed the Great Flood to cleanse the earth of evil doers. But, when done, He created a rainbow, which was His promise to never to destroy His creation, the earth, by water, ever again (Gen. 6–9). God allowed the destruction of Sodom and Gomorrah to punish the evildoers (Gen. 19:1–29). However, God relented and held His hand back (repented) from harming the evil doers of Nineveh when Jonah convinced the citizens to repent of their sins (Jonah 3). These OT passages show that God will not tolerate sin but that he is ready to forgive and relent of His wrath. This is a strict but loving God!

Remember that God will not interfere in our lives, as He gave us free will to do as we choose. However, we certainly have free will to ask Him to intervene when we need Him. He will help when the request is in line with His will for our physical and spiritual good. He created each of us as unique individuals, and He loves each one of us equally with an intense love.

Nor does He interfere with the laws of nature He created at the beginning of this universe. He certainly could, as He is all-powerful, and at times He may intervene to protect us from natural disasters. Many farmers in the Midwest share stories of tornadoes and the resulting disaster and miraculous stories of lives being saved. Victims of other natural disasters also share similar stories.

14. God and Suffering.[318] God allows suffering to bring people back to Him, whether it is suffering of the person directly or those around the person, by moving people from self-centeredness to a love for and dependence upon Him and a love for others who need care or help. The Old Testament figure Job is a prime example. He was a miserable soul. He was wealthy

---

[318]Spitzer, Fr. Robert, Essential 7: "Why Suffering?" Credible Catholic (Magis Center, www.crediblecatholic, 2017), slides 1–74.

but lost everything and even some members of his house. He fought with God. Finally, he got the word from God through a visitor that God may have been trying to purify him from his arrogance. God then gave him a vision of God's greatness and power. Job was humbled and acknowledged God's power and right to do what He chooses. God rewarded his change of heart with double the wealth and a household of sons and daughters. He lived another 140 years.[319] The message is that God is good. He has His motives and methods. We have to learn to accept them in faith, hope, and love. God's primary goal is draw us all to salvation through His Son, Jesus. Sometimes He needs to get our attention. We cannot be self-centered when it comes to His plans for us. Remember, His plan is always to help us, prosper us, and not to harm us.

Suffering helps develop a trust in God and recognition of our dependence on Him. This purifies us and deepens our love. We learn to serve Him as well as our neighbor. We begin to move along the continuum from self-centeredness to God and neighbor centeredness, which, of course, is based on love. Love is the central theme and message of the New Testament. Pain and suffering are temporary conditions in this life. We all go through it. Jesus went through it during His passion out of love for each of us, reconciling us to the Father through His death and resurrection. There has never been a greater example of suffering for the love of another than Jesus on the cross. His suffering, death, and resurrection brought us salvation! We, too, can come to salvation through belief in Jesus. This suffering and sacrifice for God and for others is out of love. We know that in Heaven, God will wipe away every tear, death shall be no more, no mourning or crying and no pain. It is a place of peace, joy, love, and no pain (Rev 21:4–5).

---

[319] Zavada, Jack, "Book of Job," ToughtCo, (www.thoughtco.com, March 7, 2017).

Remember that Jesus is always there to help us through the Holy Spirit. He healed Peter's mother-in-law and many others of their illnesses and drove our demons (Mark 1:29–39). He is all-powerful and He will help you. You just need to ask Him in humility for help. He will help you, if it is in your best interests or in the best interests of those you are praying for. Your will must align with His will. Remember, He always wants the best for you. He is a loving God!

Fr. Spitzer reminds us that God's love is confirmed by thousands of NDEs (Near Death Experience). The Beatitudes also speak to the righteousness and love of heaven for those who suffer on earth (Matt 5:1–12). Remember that suffering is necessary for most of us to grow in love.[320]

God does not directly cause suffering to punish people, nor force someone to act (we were not created as puppets), but rather, He does allow secondary causes to happen and to interact—evil people, diseases, illnesses, etc., are allowed by God.[321] But God does allow evil to cause suffering, all to our good. An interesting thought is that suffering on earth might be a very mild example of what eternal life might be like in Hell, separated from Him forever. Of course, we can never read God's mind or know why He may allow certain things to happen. All we know for certain is that He has unconditional love for each of us. He demonstrated this by His sacrifice of His only begotten son, Jesus Christ, on the cross in expiation of our sins to reunite us with Him. He may allow us to suffer here on earth; however, we can only imagine the suffering our loving God went through as His son was dying on the cross. The image of Mel Gibson's film *The Passion of the Christ* where God's tear dropped from heaven and fell on Jesus during His passion on the cross comes to mind.

---

[320]Spitzer, supra, slide 35.

[321]Id, at slide 40.

We are not called to sit idly by and suffer through whatever life throws at us. We are called to use whatever science or other technologies we have developed to reduce the suffering and to extend life on earth. And what about the power of prayer? We should always turn to Him in heartfelt prayer and ask for His help. Engage God in your situation with prayer and reduce your fear and anxiety levels, through natural abilities (prudence, reason, planning, and courage).[322] Don't try to handle your suffering alone. Have faith and trust! Turn it over to God! Try it, and you will be surprised at the power of God and His care for you, better than any science or technology—*guaranteed!* Remember, suffering can bring each of us closer to God, as strange as it may sound, by freeing us from our conceit, pride, status, and success. It humbles us. Again, remember God is not punishing those who suffer, but He only allows suffering as a reminder of Him and our dependence on him.[323]

God the Son, Jesus Christ, Our Savior

With the goal of salvation and reuniting man with God, Jesus came to earth as a human, sacrificed his human life to reconcile all humans, fallen due to original sin, back to God the Father, along with the opportunity to spend eternity in Heaven with God. There are a number of sources proving the truth of the existence of Jesus. The first is the Bible, both the Old Testament (OT) and the New Testament (NT):

a. OT and NT Scripture—prophecies of Jesus' birth, life, death, and resurrection.
b. Old Testament (OT) messianic prophesies (400+)—Forward Allusions. "These are written so that you may believe that Jesus is the Christ, the Son of God, and that by believing you

---

[322]Id, at slides 47–48.

[323]Id at slides 49–56.

may have life in His name" (John 20:31). "Now He said to them, 'These are My words which I spoke to you while I was still with you, that all things which are written about Me in the Law of Moses and the Prophets and the Psalms must be fulfilled'" (Luke 24:44). The key Biblical documentary evidence (OT references and NT fulfillment) are the following:[324]

　　i. Genesis 3:15—He will be offspring of a woman and will redeem us –Gal 4:4–5
　　ii. Genesis 12:1–3—He will be a descendant of Abraham and Isaac. Matt 1:1, 17; Heb 11:17–19
　　iii. Exodus 12:46—He will not have any of His bones broken. John 19:33–36.
　　iv. Deuteronomy 18:15—"The Lord will raise up for a prophet…" Acts 3:18-22.
　　v. 2 Samuel 7:14—"I will be his Father, and he will be my Son. When he does wrong, I will punish him with the rod, with floggings inflicted by men." Messianic prophesy of the Passion of Christ and Jesus taking on the sins of the world. Heb 1:5; 2 Cor. 5:21, 1 Peter 2:21–22.
　　vi. Psalms—variously refers to attacks against the Kingdom of God (Jesus, God the Son) and/or the Kingdom of David:
　　2:1–2, 6–7—He will be opposed by both Jews and Gentiles. He will be both King of Zion and the Son of God. Luke 1:32, 35, and 23:10–12; John 18:33–37; Acts 4:27.

---

[324]Wikipedia, "Christian Messianic Prophesies, Section 1," Prophesies Considered Fulfilled; Strobel, Lee, General Editor, *Old Testament Prophecies Fulfilled by Christ, The Case for Christ Study Bible, Investigating the Evidence for Belief* (Zondervan Publishers, 2009).

16:7–11—refers to Jesus' triumph over death, i.e., the resurrection. No bodily decay. Luke 24:6,31,34; Acts 2:24–32.

22:1–18—He will be forsaken by God, mocked by the people, pierced His hands and feet, and have his clothing divided and cast lots for His garment. Matt 27:39–44,46; Luke 22:63–65; John 19:18–20, 23–24; Rms 15:3.

34:20—"...He guards all his bones; not even one of them shall be broken." John 19:32–37.

41:9—He will be betrayed by a friend. Matt 26:14–16; Mark 14;10–11; Luke 22:1–6: John 13;18-30.

47:5—He will ascend into heaven. Luke 24:51; Acts 1:9.

69:4—He will be hated and rejected for his works. Matt 13:57; Mark 6:4; Luke 4:24; John 1:11, 7:3–5 and 5:24–25.

69:9—He will have great love for the Lord's house. John 2:17.

69:21—"... and in my thirst they gave me vinegar to drink." Matt 27:34, Mark 15:23, Luke 23:23, 36; John 19:29–30.

72:10–11—He will be adored by Magi and kings. He will have universal dominion. Nations will serve Him. Matt 2:1–11; Phil 2:9,11.

78:2—He will preach in parables. Matt 13:34–35; Mark 4:33–34.

110—messianic reference to Jesus of Nazareth. He is a priest in the order of Malchizedek; God defeating His enemies (referenced by Jesus challenging the Pharisees about the reference to Him and not David. Col 3:1; Heb 1:3, 5:5–6; Matt 22:41–46.

118:22—He will be rejected by the Jewish rulers. Matt 21:42; Mark 12:10; Luke 20:17; 1 Peter 2:4–7.

vii. Wisdom 2:12–20—Solomon's speech to the rulers of the earth urging them to love righteousness and seek wisdom. Prophesized the coming of a righteous man, calling himself the Son of God, who would suffer at the hands of the people and die a shameful death.[325] Passion narratives in Matthew 26–28, Mark 14–15, Luke 22–23, and John 18–19.

viii. Isaiah 7:14—Isaiah addressing King Ahaz of Judah promises that God will destroy his enemies (Assyrian army); a young virgin will give birth to the child Immanuel (God is with us); Book of Isaiah quoted many times by New Testament authors (John 12:41), including the Suffering Servant.[326] Matt 1:21–23; Luke 2:7.

8:14—He will be a stumbling block to those who refuse to believe in Him – Luke 2:34; Rms 9:32–33; 1 Peter 2:8.

9:2–7—"The people who have sat in darkness have seen a great light." He will have a ministry that begins in Galilee. He will have an everlasting kingdom. Matt 4:12–16, 23; Luke 1:32–33.

9:6—"For a child is born unto us, a son will be given to us. And the government will rest on His shoulders, and His name will be called Wonderful, Counselor, the Mighty God, The Everlasting Father, the Prince of Peace." Luke 2:1–15; Matt 1:18–2:23.

---

[325]Wikipedia, "Book of Wisdom," Section 1, Structure, Genre and Content.

[326]Wikipedia, "Isaiah," Section 2, in Christianity.

11:10; 42:1—State of Israel; inclusion of Gentiles into the people of God. John 10:16; Acts 10:34–35, 45, 47.

35:5–6—He will perform miracles. Matt 11:4–6; John 9:6,7.

40:3—He will be preceded by an anointed messenger. Matt 3;13; Mark 1:2–3; Luke 1:12, 76–77, 3;3–6; John 1:23-32He will be meek and speak out for justice. Matt 12:15–21.

50:6—He will be spat on and beaten. Matt 26:67; Mark 14:65, 15:19; John 19:1–5.

53:1–12, 3–9,12[327]—most famous of the Isaiah messianic prophesies, the Suffering Servant who suffers because of the sins of others "But he was wounded (pierced) for our transgressions, he was bruised for our iniquities: the chastisement of our peace was upon him, and with his stripes we are healed." We have gone astray. The iniquity of all was laid on Him; He was tortured butt never opened His mouth; He was assigned a grave with the wicked and rich in death, yet he did no violence; He bore the sin of many, and made intercession for the transgressors. Matt 26:62–63, 27:11–14, 27–50, 57–60; Mark 15:4–5, 21–37, 42–46; Luke 23:6–9, 32–46, 50–53; John 19:16–30, 38–42; 1 Peter 2:22.

61:1—He will be anointed by the Spirit of God. Matt 3–16; Mark 1:10; Luke 3:22, 4:16–19; John 3:34, 5:30; Acts 10:38; Rev 19:11.

61:1-2 – He will enter into public ministry. Luke 4;16-21, 43

---

[327]Stoebel, Lee, *The Case for Christ: A Journalist's Personal Investigation of the Evidence for Jesus Christ* (Zondervan, Harper and Collin Publishers, 2017), 54–55.

ix. Jerimiah 31:15—refers to the captivity of Rachel's children in Assyria and prophetically to King Herod's slaughter of the innocents. Matt 2:16–18.
x. Ezekiel 37:26–27—Sanctuary/Temple/dwelling place refers to the messiah as a messianic temple. 1 Cor 3:16.
xi. Daniel 9:24–27—references to "most holy," "anointed (messiah)," and "prince" are considered to refer to Jesus. Mark 13:14; Matt 24:15.
xii. Hosea 11:1—The son of Israel, being called out of Egypt, refers to Jesus coming back out of Egypt with Mary and Joseph. Matt 2:15.
xii. Micah 5:2–5—prophesied the birth of Jesus in Bethlehem. Matt 2:1–6; Luke 2:4–7.
xiv. Haggai 2:6–9—references a Second Temple/new house is to be filled with the glory of God; it references Jesus.
xv. Zechariah 9:9—"Rejoice greatly, O daughter of Zion! Shout in triumph, O daughter of Jerusalem! Behold, your king is coming to you; He is just and endowed with salvation, Humble, and mounted on a donkey, Even on a colt, the foal of a donkey." John 12:13–1; Matt 21:1–5. In most ancient Jewish writings, this passage applied to the Messiah.[328]

11:12–13—Thirty pieces of silver thrown to the potter in the house of the Lord. Matt 26:15, 27:7.

12:10—"And I will pour upon the house of David, and upon the inhabitants of Jerusalem, the spirit of grace and of supplication; and they shall look unto Me because they have thrust him through;

---

[328] Wikipedia, "Christian Messianic Prophesy," Section 1, Prophesies Considered Fulfilled.

and they shall mourn for him, as one mourns for his only son, and shall be in bitterness for him, as one that is in bitterness for his first-born." Messianic prophesy of the crucifixion and death of Jesus. John 19:34, 32–37.

13:7—He will be forsaken by His disciples. Matt 26:31, 56.

    xvi. Malachi 3:1—He will arrive at Jerusalem's temple. Matt 21:12; Mark 11:11; Luke 19:45–48; John 2:13–16.

c. New Testament (NT)—Biblical evidence of Jesus' dual nature - humanity and divinity.[329] Trent Horn lays out an excellent outline of proof as to the truth of Jesus as the living Son of God the Father:

    i. Archangel Gabriel appears to Mary to announce the God would favor her with a new son, Immanuel (God is with us). He is to be called Jesus. Mary agreed. Luke 1:28–36.

    ii. Jesus becomes human. John 1:14.

    iii. God calls Jesus His Son. Matt 3:13–17; Mark 1:9–11; Luke 3:21–22.

    iv. Jesus is called God and refers to himself as God. John 1:1, 5:20; Titus 2:13; Col 2:9; Heb 1:5–8; 2 Ptr 1:1; John 8:58; 1 John 1.

    v. Jesus acts like God. Mark 2:5-7, Luke 22:29, John 8:58–59.

    vi. Jesus is honored and worshipped like God. John 20:28, Phil 2:5-11; Heb 1:6–8; Matt 14:33; Mark 5:6; Jn 9:38.

    vii. Jesus given all the authority in Heaven and Earth. Matthew 28:18–20.

---

[329]Horn, supra, at p 47.

viii. Jesus teachings – Jesus gave us the New Greatest Commandment – Love God with all your heart, mind, and soul, and love your neighbor as yourself – all about love. Matt 22:35–40; Mark 12:28–34; Luke 10:25–28; this commandment is all about God the Father and one another. Jesus points to everyone else but Himself in total humility and servant leadership. He paid the ultimate price by dying on the cross for each of usf us proving his deep love for humanity—

ix. Alphabetical listing of Jesus miracles performed during his lifetime, which are all verifiable[330]:
  1. A second net of fish. John 21:1–2.
  2. Calming the stormy waters. Mark 4:35–41; Matt 8:18–27; Luke 8:22–25.
  3. Casting demons out of lunatic boy. Mark 9:14–29; Matt 17:14–21; Luke 9:37–42.
  4. Casting out a dumb and blind spirit. Luke 11:14–26, Matt 12:22–32, Mark 3:22–30.
  5. Casting out a spirit. Matt 9:32–34.
  6. Cleansing a leper. Mark 1:40–45; Matt 8:1–4.
  7 Cleansing 10 lepers. Luke 17:11–19.
  8. Cursing the fig tree. Mark 11:12–26.
  9. Delivering a man in the synagogue from demonic spirits. Mark 1:21–28; Luke 4:31–37.
  10. Delivering the Syrophonecian daughter. Matt 15:21–28.
  11. Feeding 5,000 with five loaves and two fish. John 6:1–14; Matt 14:13–21; Mark 6:32–34; Luke 9:10–13.

---

[330]Foundation Mary Pages Design, "The 35 Miracles of Jesus with Scripture References," www.marypages.com/MiraclesJesus.html (December 2017).

12. Feeding another 4,000. Mark 8:1–10; Matt 15:32.
13. Healing the deaf and dumb man. Mark 7:31–37.
14. Healing the man born blind. John 9:1–41.
15. Healing the possessed man at Gadara. Mark 5:1–20; Matt 8:28; Luke:26.
16. Healing man with withered hand. Luke 6:6–11; Matt 12:9–13; Mark 3:1–5.
17. Healing a man with dropsy (edema). Luke 14:1–6.
18. Healing a paralytic. Mark 2:1–12; Matt 9:2-8; Luke 5;17–26.
19. Healing a woman with an 18 year infirmity. Luke 13:10–17.
20. Healing a woman with a blood issue. Mark 5;25–34; Matt 9:18–26; Luke 8:40–56.
21. Healing blind Bartimeaus. Mark 10:46–52.
22. Healing a nobleman's son. John 4:46–52.
23. Healing of Malchus's ear. Luke 49:51–52.
24. Healing of the man at Bathesda. John5:1–15.
25. Healing of two blind men. Matt 9:27–31.
26. Healing Peter's mother in law. Mark 1:29–31; Luke 4:38–39; Matt 8:14–15.
27. Healing the blind man at Bethsaida. Mark 8:22–26.
28. Healing the Centurion's servant. Luke 7:1–10.
29. Pulling a coin form the fish's mouth. Matt 17:24–27.
30. Raising Jairus' daughter. Mark 5:21–43.
31. Raising Lazarus. John 11:1–46.
32. Raising the widow's son. Luke 7:11–16.
33. The first two nets of fish. Luke 5:1–11.
34. Turning water into wine. John 2:1–11.

35. Walking on water. Matt 14:22–33; John 6:15–21; Matt 6:45–52.
x. Jesus betrayed by Judas for 30 pieces of silver. Matt 26:15; 27:5,7.
xi. Jesus said He would be raised from the dead in three days. Matt 27:63; Mark 8:31, and John 2:19–21. Jesus raised from the dead three days later (Friday to Sunday). Matt 28:1–9; Mark 16:1–8; Luke 24:1–8; Acts 2:32. Jesus' resurrection from the dead is the greatest miracle God has ever given humankind! This miracle proves the supernatural power of our God and proves that resurrection from the dead and spiritual eternal life is also our destiny.
xii. Two angels at the tomb telling Mary and Mary Magdalene that Jesus is not there.[331] Matt 28:1–8; Mark 16:1–8; Luke 24:1–10; John 20:1–8. Jesus has arisen from the dead!
xiii. Post Resurrection Appearances. Jesus appeared to His 12 apostles; then to 500 followers at the same time; then to Thomas who put his hand into Jesus' side; then to James, and finally to Paul on the road. 1 Cor 15:3–8.[332]
   1. To Mary Magdalene. John 20:10–18.
   2. To other women. Matt 28:8–10.
   3. To Cleopas and another traveler on way to Emmaus. Luke 24:13–32.
   4. To eleven disciples and others. Luke 24:33–49.
   5. To ten apostles and others with Thomas absent. John 20;19–23.
   6. To Thomas and the other apostles. John 26–30.

---

[331]Stoebel, supra at Chapter 8, "What Happened to the Body," pp. 117–132.

[332]Strobel, supra at p. 137.

7. To seven apostles. John 21:16–20.
8. To the disciples. Matt 28:16–20.
9. To the apostles at the Mount of Olives. Luke 24:50–52 and Acts 1:4–9.

xiv After His resurrection, Jesus finally fulfills the OT prophecies, which He explained to His followers. Luke 24:44–49; Acts 1:6–8.

xv. Jesus worshipped again after resurrection. Jn 20:27:28; Mt 28:9, 17; Lk 24:51.

xvi. The four gospel writers were contemporaries of Jesus and recorded events as they saw them.

xvii. 24,000 original copies of the New Testament copied in different languages with 99.5% accuracy.[333]

Note that all these miracles have a unique quality about them:[334]

i. He performs them by His own authority.
ii. Their purpose was to bring the kingdom of God the Father into the world—pointing toward salvation and eternal life—and not His own glory.
iii. They always heal or deliver a person from a demonic state of evil—displaying the love of God.
iv. Many are a basis of teaching of the Good News of God's love and the opportunity for salvation.
v. The faith and free choice of the individual are always an integral part.
vi. Jesus shows his power to forgive sins as a confessor of God—a precursor to his death for all sins of man reconciling us to God the Father.

---

[333] Strobel, Lee, supra at p 79.

[334] Spitzer, Fr Robert, "Essential 4: Proof of Jesus' Resurrection," Credible Catholic (Magis Center, www.crediblecatholic.com, 2017) slides 7–8.

For those readers who are looking at other monotheistic religions or even polytheistic religions, I hope that you consider the strength of these many supernatural miracles to believe in the Christian God again. Miracles are often used by religions of every type to prove the truth of the supernatural powers. Christianity has by far and away the vast majority of proven miracles, including the most significant miracle ever – Jesus' resurrection from the dead. No other faith or religion can claim any true miracles including resurrection from the dead!

d. Non-biblical historical evidence:[335]
      i. Titus Flavius Josephus (AD 37–101)—first-century Jewish historian—said Jesus was a wise man that Pontius Pilate condemned to a Roman death on a cross.
      ii. Cornelius Tacitus (AD 54–120)—second-century Roman historian—said Christians received their name from Christus who was put to death by Pontius Pilate, Procurator of Judea in the reign of Tiberius. He recorded Jesus' teaching to His disciples, Pilate's sentence of Jesus to crucifixion, His death, resurrection and appearance to his disciples three days later. Josephus reported on the new movement started by Jesus and opined that perhaps Jesus was the sought-after Messiah.[336]. (Note that Tacitus could be treated as a hostile witness in a court of law as he spoke condescendingly and

---

[335] Id; Josephus, *Antiquities of the Jews*, 18.3.3 and 20.9.1; Tacitus, *Annals*, 15.44; Bart Ehrman, *Did Jesus Exist? The Historical Argument for Jesus of Nazareth* (New York: Harperone, 2012), 4; Spitzer, Fr Robert, "Essential 4: Proof of Jesus' Resurrection," Credible Catholic (Magis Center, www.crediblecatholic.com, 2017), slides 13–14.

[336] Id.; Josephus, Antiquities, XVIII, 63.

perniciously about Jesus and was not a friend of Christ or the disciples, adding to his credibility in support of Christ existing).[337]

  iii. Suetonius (AD 69–120)—another respected historian and biographer specializing in Roman emperors—Claudius (reigned AD 41–54) expelled the Christian movement from Rome.[338]
  iii. Bart Ehrman (1959–)—contemporary agnostic scholar—says that virtually every expert on earth knows that Jesus existed.[339]

e. Biblical documentary evidence—Jesus Birth, Death and Resurrection:

1. Corroborating Evidence—Birth:
i. Virgin conception and birth—Archangel Gabriel prophesized and announced virgin birth to Mary.
ii. OT—Gabriel appeared to Daniel to prophesy the coming of a Messiah. Daniel 8:15–19 and 9:20–27.
iii. NT—Gabriel appears to Zacharias to announce birth of St John the Baptist to Elizabeth to announce way of the Lord. Luke 1:8–24.
iv. NT—Gabriel appears to Mary to announce the birth of Jesus; Luke 1:26–38. Mary responds with the Magnificat while meeting with Elizabeth. Luke 1:46–55.
v. NT—Gabriel appears to Joseph in a dream explaining the significance of the birth of Immanuel. Matt 1:18–25.

---

[337] Oborn, Ragnar, Consider Design, Part 4, Consider the Gospel, (considerthegospel.com, vimeo.com); Tacitus, Annals XV, 44 Roman Historian, 116 AD.

[338] Oborn, supra; Suetonius, Claudius XXV, 4.

[339] Wikipedia, Bart D. Ehrman, Career.

vi. Jesus' Birth—Physical evidence of cave and eye witnesses: guiding star, angels, shepherds and three Kings proven to come from the area of and Persia, Arabia, and India.[340]
2. Further Corroborating Evidence—Life and Teaching:
i. NT references to his youth and middle age—scarce historical reports prior to His ministry starting at age 30.
ii. NT references to teachings—the essence of the Gospels of Matthew Mark, Luke, and John.
iii. NT references to miracles (see summaries above).
iv. Eye witnesses (Peter, John, and James) to transfiguration on Mt. Tabor and discussions with Moses and Elijah. Matt 17:1–13; Mark 9:2–8; and Luke 9:29.
v. Further support in the Acts of the Apostles (St Paul), Apocrypha, and Letters from His Apostles focused on the salvation messages of Jesus.
3. Further Corroborating Evidence—Real Evidence and the Bible, Death, NT references to Passion:
    i. Jesus statement to Pontius Pilate when asked if He was the Son of God. Jesus responded "I am."
    ii. Roman sign on the cross—"INRI"—"This is the King of the Jews."
    iii. Physical evidence of Garden of Gethsemane and Golgotha.
    iv. Gethsemane still exists with 2,000 year-old olive trees.
    v. Golgotha has been covered by Muslim, Jewish, and Catholic shrines—Temple Mount.

4. Scientific medical evidence of Jesus' death on the cross. Current medical science was consulted on the flogging, crown of thrones, carrying the cross, nailing to the cross, asphyxiation,

---

[340] Wikipedia, "Biblical Magi, Names and Country of Origin and Journey."

lancing of Jesus' right side with a spear and the water and blood that flowed out are all proven as Roman means of torture and execution. These insults to the body were obviously enough to kill the body. The flow of blood and water from the lungs prove the death by asphyxiation. Jesus died on the cross.[341]

5. Physical real evidence of Jesus' death and resurrection—Shroud of Turin and Facecloth of Oviedo—matches a man of 5'7" to 6'2" tall, with shoulder length hair, beard, and mustache. The wounds in one wrist and feet, flogging scourge marks on the back, swollen face, spear wound in the right side, streams of blood down the face from a crown of thorns are indicative of a Roman crucifixion as described in the Gospels. The eyes were covered with Roman Leptons, minted by Pontius Pilate in Judea in AD 29. The Shroud was Carbon-14 dated to about AD 33, the time of Jesus' death. Pollen grains in the cloth were determined to be mostly from the Sea of Galilee region. The blood on the Shroud was type tested to AB+ (very rare), and was beneath the image. The Facecloth of Oviedo was similarly tested, and the scientists found 120 matches with the Shroud of Turin, including pollen origin, blood type, and facial features. The image is limited to the top layers of cloth indicating intense light radiation. Because even the interior bone structure matched the flesh, scientists are of the opinion that the very high energy radiation blast singing the cloth, emanated equally from every part of the body and the cloth collapsed through the body, i.e., instantaneous transfiguration and resurrection of the body (such as we shall experience at the final judgment), giving a three-dimensional image of Jesus![342]

---

[341]Edwards, Dr. William, et al., "On the Physical Death of Jesus Christ," JAMA, 1986; 255:1455–63.

[342]Spitzer, supra at slides 18-47

6. Corroborating Evidence—Bible Historicity, Resurrection:
i. Physical evidence of Sepulcher Tomb and angels—testimony of Mary Magdalene and Mary the mother of Joses reported in NT scripture.
ii. Appeared to Peter, then the twelve, then to the 500 eye witnesses who were still alive, then to James and again to the apostles, and finally to Paul who writes of these accounts. 1 Corinthians 15:3–8.
iii. Apostles witness ascension into Heaven. Luke 24:50–52; Mark 16:19–20; Acts 1–11.
7. Direct Evidence—Bible Historicity, Post Resurrection Appearances:[343]
i. Women at the empty tomb. Matt 28:8–10.
ii. Mary Magdalene at the empty tomb. John 20:11–18.
iii. Apostle Peter. Luke 24:34.
iv. Ten disciples. John 20:19–25.
v. Eleven disciples (including Thomas). John 20:26–29.
vi. 500 followers. 1 Cor 15:6.
vii. Apostle James. 1 Cor 15:7.
viii. Group of disciples at the Sea of Galilee. John 21:1–23.
ix. Two followers on the road to Emmaus. Luke 24:13–32.
x. Disciples at His ascension. Matt 28:16–20.
xi. Saul on the road to Damascus. Acts 9:3–6.

f. Character of Jesus.[344]
    1. Omniscient—All-knowing (John 16:30).
    2. Omnipresent—Present everywhere at the same time (Matt 28:20).

---

[343]Strobel, Lee, General Editor, Resurrection Appearances of Jesus, The Case for Christ Study Bible, Investigating the Evidence for Belief (Zondervan Publishers, Grand Rapids MI, 2009).

[344]Strobel, Lee, *The Case for Christ: A Journalist's Personal Investigation of the Evidence for Jesus* (Sondervan, Harper Collins Publishers, 2017), p 27.

3. Omnipotent—All authority in Heaven and earth (Matt 28:18).
4. Eternal—Jesus was with God from the beginning (John 1:1).
5. Immutable—Unchanging (Heb 13:8).
6. Gave life for all mankind—"I am the way, the truth and the life. No one comes to the Father except through me" (John 14:6).
7. He is a relational God and loves each one of us with an unimaginable love—believe, repent and confess your sins and love Him and your neighbor as yourself. Jesus, God the Son, restored that relationship through his life, death and resurrection (Luke 19:10, Romans 5:8–10, Col 1:19–22).

g. Post NT Physical Proof of Jesus' Divinity and eternal life with Him in Heaven:
1. Shroud of Turin – real evidence – AB+ blood (rarest type)
2. Miracle of Transformed Host and Wine at Lanciano, Italy, (700s) and Sienna, Italy, (1730), and most recently in Buenos Aires, Argentina, (1996)—real evidence—AB+ blood and heart tissue.[345]

h. Post NT Evidence and Proof of Jesus' Divinity, Death and Resurrection:
1. Appearances of Blessed Virgin Mary – points to salvation through her Son, Jesus – eye witness accounts. Of over 1,500 reported apparitions, here are 10 apparitions approved as authentic by the Catholic Church:

---

[345] Spitzer, Fr Robert, "Essential 5: Why be Catholic?" Credible Catholic (Magis Center, www.crediblecatholic.com, 2017), slides 32–42.

a. Teypeyac, Mexico City, Villa de Guadalupe, Mexico, 1531. Appearance to Juan Diego, roses (testamentary evidence), Mary's image on his tilma (real evidence) to the bishop to help him believe. Subsequently, he started construction of the basilica that still stands with the tilma hanging at the altar uncorrupted for nearly 500 years.[346]
b. Laus, France to Benoite Rencurel, shepherdess, 1665–1718.
c. Rue de Bac, Paris to St Catherine Leboure', 1830.
d. LaSalette, France, to two shepherd children, Melanie Calvat and Maximim Giraud, 1846.
e. Lourdes, France, to St Bernadette Soubirous, 1858, appeared to St Bernadette (testamentary evidence) many reported healing subsequently.
f. Pontmain, France, to a number of young children, 1871.
g. Knock, County of Mayo, Ireland, to 15 men women and children, 1879.
h. Fatima, Portugal, 1917, appeared to three shepherd children, Lucia, Francisco, and Jacinta and later 30,000–100,000 witnesses including agnostic press
i. Miracle of the spinning sun
ii. Miracle of dried clothing after rainstorm. Mary shared three prophecies about 1) vision of Hell, 2) end of WW I, and the consecration of Russia to her name, and 3) the death of a Pope.[347]

---

[346]Id, slides 49–57.

[347]Wikipedia, "Our Lady of Fatima."

      i. Beauraing, Belgium to five children, 33 visions, 1932.

      j. Banneux, Belgium to young child Mariette Beco, 8 visions, 1933[348]. Medjugorje, Bosnia, 1981, Mary appeared to six children. Miraculous visions of the sun are reported. Pope Francis has declared the visions worth studying in more detail, but they are not yet worthy of belief.[349]

2. Stigmata—Recorded Testimony and Photographs (Exceptions to Hearsay Rule). There is documented proof of at least 321 stigmatics worthy of belief, 62 saints with stigmata, and 20 stigmatics in the twentieth century.[350] Here are most recognized for their stigmata:

    a. St. Francis, Italy, (1181–1226), 1224, received the five stigmata (wounds of Christ).[351]

    b. St. Padre Pio, (1887–1968), 1918, received five stigmata.[352]

    c. St. Catherine of Sienna, Italy, (1347–1380), 1375, initially visible stigmata, but St Catherine prayed that they be made invisible during her life out of humility, and God granted her wish.[353]

---

[348]Foundation Mary Pages, "The Apparitions of the Blessed Virgin Mary," www.marypages.com (December 2017); Wikipedia, "Marian Apparition."

[349]Wikipedia, "Our Lady of Medjugorje."

[350]"Mystical Stigmata," New Advent, Catholic Encyclopedia (www.newadvent.org, 2017).

[351]"The Stigmata of Saint Francis Assisi, 1224" (catholicism.org, Sept 27, 2000).

[352]Wikipedia, "Padre Pio, Stigmata."

[353]"Mystical Stigmata," supra.

However they were visible in her corpse after death.
3. Incorruptibles—Real Evidence and Photographic Records. Bodies are remarkably preserved supernaturally. Catholics believe this is a miraculous sign of their holiness with a saintly life. Catholics recognize over 120 incorruptible saints/blessed.[354] Distinguished from embalming and mummification. [355] Some of the more recognized saints:
   a. St Bernadette Sobirous (1844–1879)
   b. St Catherine of Sienna (1347–1380)
   c. St Padre Pio (1887–1968)
   d. St John Vianney (1786–1859)

God the Holy Spirit—Communicator/Dwells in your Heart. The Holy Spirit has also existed from the beginning of time with the Father and the Son. Physical evidence, Bible, and other documentary testimonial evidence recorded.[356]
1. Conception of Jesus: Mary conceived Jesus through the Holy Spirit. Matthew 1:18–25 and Luke 1:26–38. Nicene and Apostles' Creed.
2. Baptism of Jesus: Holy Spirit in the form of a dove descends on Jesus during His Baptism in the Jordan River by John the Baptist, witnessed by others. God declared audibly to the crowds "this is my beloved Son in whom I am well pleased." Matt 3:13–17; Mark 1:9–11; Luke 3:21–23. The historicity of

---

[354]"The Incorruptible Saints, Roman Catholic Saints," (www.roman-catholic-saints.com).

[355]Wikipedia, "Incorruptibility."

[356]Wikipedia, "Holy Spirit."

John the Baptist performing the baptism is well established scripturally and historically.[357]
3. Pentecost: Holy Spirit in the form of tongues of fire descended on the 11 Apostles and other disciples in upper room. They began speaking in tongues at Pentecost, 50 days after Easter and 10 days after the Ascension into Heaven, witnessed by 100s. About 3,000 repented and were baptized in the name of Jesus. Acts 2:1–47.[358]
i. Pentecost was the beginning of Jesus' church. 1 Tim 3:15.
4. Significance of Holy Spirit to Christians—The Holy Spirit will also come into our spirits and help us. Paul exhorts:

"Therefore brethren, we are debtors, not to the flesh to live according to the flesh, for if you live according to the flesh you will die, but if by the Spirit you put to death the deeds of the body, you will live. For as many as are led by the Spirit of God, these are sons of God" (Romans 8:12–13).

With the help of the Holy Spirit you can overcome sin. Set aside the physical lusts of the heart and replace it with the love of God—the Holy Spirit will indwell in your heart and spirit and be there to help you through the ups and downs of life. It will take suffering and effort to purify yourself from old habits, but the rewards will be eternal! Paul reminds the followers:

---

[357] Id; Wikipedia, "Baptism of Jesus"; *The Gospel of Matthew* by Daniel J. Harrington 1991 ISBN 0-8146-5803-2 p. 63; "Christianity: A Biblical, Historical, and Theological Guide" by Glenn Jonas, Kathryn Muller Lopez 2010, pp. 95–96; *Studying the Historical Jesus: Evaluations of the State of Current Research* by Bruce Chilton, Craig A. Evans 1998 ISBN 90-04-11142-5 pp. 187–98; *Jesus as a Figure in History: How Modern Historians View the Man from Galilee* by Mark Allan Powell 1998 ISBN 0-664-25703-8 p. 47; Craig Evans, "Josephus on John the Baptist" in *The Historical Jesus in Context* edited by Amy-Jill Levine et al. Princeton Univ Press 20060, 55–58. ISBN 978-0-691-00992-6.

[358] Wikipedia, "Pentecost."

> "Walk in the Spirit and *you* shall not fulfill the lusts of the flesh." Galatians 5:16

Praying to the Holy Spirit, the third Person of the Trinity, is the same as praying to God the Father and Jesus, God the Son. Your prayers are fully united. The Trinity hears your prayers. As the Holy Spirit to come into your spirit/soul and dwell within you. Pray to Him for help in all circumstances.

Know the spirit of truth:

> "And I will pray the Father, and He will give you another Helper, that He may abide with you forever—the Spirit of truth, whom the world cannot receive, because it neither sees Him nor knows Him; but you know Him, for He dwells with you and will be in you. I will not leave you orphans; I will come to you" John 14:16–18. (See also Acts 1:4–5.)

He will answer.

> "Now may the God of hope fill you with all joy and peace in believing, that you may abound in hope by the power of the Holy Spirit." Romans 15:13. [359]

5. Blessings—We have been blessed by certain gifts from the Holy Spirit, which make us better Christians and draws us closer to God and each other, fulfilling the great Commandments of Jesus: Love God with all your heart mind and soul and love your neighbor as yourself. Our spiritual goal is salvation and eternal life with Him. We are graced with the help of God. He acts through the Holy Spirit.

---

[359] Albig, Kathryn, "Do You Understand How Important Pentecost is?" Edification, Active Christianity, (http://activechristianity.org/understand-significant-pentecost).

According to the Catholic Tradition (CCC), the **gifts of the Holy Spirit** are:[360]

a. **Wisdom**—First and greatest of fruits. Holy Spirit will instill knowledge in your intellect to help direct your will toward Jesus and others—corresponds to the virtue of **charity**.
b. **Understanding**—Intuition to illuminate the mind to grasp the truths of faith; perfects theological virtue of **faith**.
c. **Counsel**—intuition that allows person to make right judgment in difficult situations; perfects cardinal virtue of **prudence**. Prudence acts with reason as enlightened by faith through the Holy Spirit to illuminate the will of God.
d. **Fortitude**—courage and fortitude to stand up for righteousness even in the face of abuse, rejection and physical harm; perfects the cardinal virtue of **courage**.
e. **Knowledge**—allows one to see, from a human perspective, things from God's perspective, His greatness and His love; perfects the theological virtue of **faith**.
f. **Piety/Reverence**—we come before God in reverence recognizing total reliance on Him, and in total humility, trust and love causing us to increase our love for Him and for others; fulfills the virtue of **justice**.
g. **Fear of the Lord**—we are not fearful of the Lord's anger or wrath but rather fearful of separation from Him as our Father, Abba, Papa, Daddy; perfects the theological virtue of **hope**.

These gifts "...complete and perfect the virtues of those who receive them."[361]

---

[360] Wikipedia, "Seven Gifts of the Holy Spirit"; CCC 1831.

[361] Id.

The **nine fruits of the Holy Spirit** come from the gifts.[362] The Catholic Church explains that they are very significant in our faith walk. They are:

a. **Love**—St Paul provides a good definition: "Love is patient, love is kind. It does not envy, it does not boast, it is not proud. It does not dishonor others, it is not self-seeking, it is not easily angered, it keeps no record of wrongs. Love does not delight in evil but rejoices with the truth. It always protects, always trusts, always hopes, always perseveres. Love never fails. But where there are prophecies, they will cease; where there are tongues, they will be stilled; where there is knowledge, it will pass away;"[363]
b. **Joy**—Happiness centered on God;
c. **Peace**—Lack of national, local and personal conflict; state of quietness, rest and sense of wholeness and wellbeing; tranquility, harmony; in spirituality, a soul assured of salvation through Christ;
d. **Patience**—long-suffering and endurance; patient endurance; slow to anger and rich in kindness;
e. **Kindness**—acting for the good and wellbeing of other people without expectation of return; goodness, sweetness and gentleness in disposition and in dealing with others;
f. **Goodness (Generosity)**—state of being good; moral excellence; kindness, generosity;
g. **Faithfulness**—trustworthy, responsible, faithful believers in Jesus and salvation He brings;
h. **Gentleness**—even-tempered, tranquil, calm, humble and self-controlled, bearing with others in love; and
i. **Self-control**—able to control one's thoughts and actions.

---

[362]Wikipedia, "Fruit of the Holy Spirit"; Gal 5:22–23.

[363]Cor 14:4–8.

Notice that all of these fruits are founded in the Love of Christ—the fulfillment of His Great Commandments: love God with all your heart, mind and strength and your neighbor as yourself.

God the Holy Spirit's Character: The Holy Spirit epitomizes the intense love between the Father and Son and between the Father and Son and each of us. He watches over each of us. He is the messenger and communicator between us and Heaven. He is our conscience and constantly communicates with us through that conscience. He changes hearts through gentle persuasion. He helps us know and obey the Ten Commandments of the OT and the Two Greatest Commandments of Jesus in the NT.

The Holy Trinity—The Father, Son, and Holy Spirit acting together consubstantially in perfect unity constitute the Trinity. Evidence of The Holy Trinity is presented primarily through reason derived from both direct and circumstantial evidence, and from inferences in Sacred Scripture and conceptual adoption in the Sacred Tradition of the Church. There is no scripture proving the concept of the Trinity, other than the command to baptize followers in the name of the Father, Son and Holy Spirit (Mark 28:19). This is a matter of faith. It is very difficult for the human mind to embrace the infinite mind and knowledge of the three consubstantial Persons of the Trinity. We can only grasp at snippets of understanding the infinite magnificence, power, love, and whole character of God and leave the Trinity, and infer and reason the Trinity. Let's start with what we know from our sources:

Father—First Person of the Trinity. Creator. We know from all the evidence presented above that God the Father is the creator and ultimate source of all that exists in this physical world and by extension all that exists in other dimensions and worlds. We know, by reason, He preceded the Big Bang, because without a supernatural intelligent design force behind the Big Bang, there would not have been the matter and order we see in the universe. Some claim that the Big Bang could have happened spontaneously without creation or design. I challenge them with the following questions, "And how exactly could that have happened? Something from nothing? Spontaneously out of what matter? Logically, wouldn't someone or something have had to create the infinite mass (both visible and invisible) we know as our four-dimensional universe (including time)?" Additional questions: "What about Heaven, the spiritual realm? We know it exists from scripture and Church tradition, personal observation, and hard evidence. Who or what created that? And to what end?" As mentioned above, the Father is all-knowing, all-intelligent, all-powerful, and all-loving, etc. He is the unquestionable truth behind creation, both physical and spiritual! He is the "cause." He is in all and is all! Only God the Father could have created the universe through his omnipotence. And he created earth and everything on it including humankind.

God gave us the Ten Commandments in the OT, with strict and clear direction of how to conduct oneself in a manner pleasing to the Father, to help order our lives back to Him. This was part of His ultimate plan to help us with our lives here on earth and ultimately to reconcile mankind to Himself, through the sacrifice of His Son so that we might spend eternity with Him in Heaven.

Son—Second Person of the Trinity. Savior. We know from evidence presented above that sacred scripture and church tradition correctly concludes that God the Father created (begot) Jesus Christ, God the Son, to exist with Him in Heaven in continuing glory and in love. That is God's nature and character. He is so loving that He wanted companions that he could love eternally and commune with. Jesus is that creation. That is why He is referred to in scripture as God, the Son, the second person of the Holy Trinity. And God the Son has had a purpose, assisting God the Father in fighting evil in Heaven and on earth. Satan and his dominion of one third of the angels who rebelled against God were evil in Heaven. They were expelled by God to spend eternity away from Him in Hell. God has loosed Satan on earth. Satan has temporary authority to roam the earth searching for souls to drag into Hell. And humans, created by God the Father, have the free will to choose either good or evil. Remember God is always there to help us withstand the temptations of Satan. But we must ask Him for that help because we all have free will. He will not interfere with our free will unless we ask.

Jesus' primary purpose was to bring the opportunity for salvation to the fallen human race (caused by the original sin of Adam and Eve through the temptations of Satan). Jesus brings salvation to us through justification, through His life, death, and resurrection. With His selfless sacrifice, he reconciled us to the Father, giving us each the opportunity to choose the good way and ultimately heaven. He offered to become one of us, even though fully divine in nature, and to take on a human body, and even to ultimately die for us for the forgiveness of our sins, which had created the chasm between us and the Father. The doors to heaven, which had been closed for millennia, were now again open to receive us at death. He sacrificed all, out of pure love for the human race. This is the same love experienced between the Father and the Son. He was willing to give everything for our salvation and communion with Him in Heaven for eternity. This is the effort to reconcile a fallen world back to the Father. Jesus, the Son, epitomizes in a human way the true meaning of love. He gave us the Greatest Commandment in the NT, based entirely on the love of God and love of neighbor.

Holy Spirit—Third person of the Trinity. Indweller and Communicator. We derive proof of His existence presented above both from circumstantial and direct evidence. The essence of the Holy Spirit is love. He is the creation of the Father and the Son to embody the perfect love between them. When Jesus, the Son, was resurrected, He shared the Holy Spirit with us at Pentecost, to remain with us to the end of time. We characterize Him as the Great Communicator, the essence of love between each of us and the Trinity as well as between us and our neighbors. He is consubstantial with the Father and the Son. He epitomizes the love in the relationship between Father and Son, and Heaven and earth. I believe His primary function to be relational. He watches over us, shares our prayers with the Father and Son, and guides us toward salvation and eternal life with the Trinity. God is love! This love is fruitful. The Holy Spirit shares His gifts and fruits with each of us.

The Holy Trinity—Sacred Tradition and Doctrine[364] teaches us that the Holy Trinity consists of God the Father, God the Son, and God the Holy Spirit—three distinct persons but one body with different purposes and spiritual functions acting in complete unison with one another. (Matt. 28:19; Mark 1:9–11; John 1:1–14 and 14:16–17).[365] One God in three persons—consubstantial, i.e., one nature and one substance.[366] Each of us is the beneficiary of this love in the story of creation.

Hopefully you now have enough scriptural, scientific, historical, and testimonial proof of the existence of God the Father, God the Son, and God the Holy Spirit to regain your trust, faith, and belief in God. It is so important that you believe and trust in God. Your eternity depends on it. I pray that you choose God over Satan.

---

[364] CCC 232-36, 249-56, and 257–67.

[365] Washer, Paul David, *The One True God* (Granted Ministries Press, 3rd Ed, 2009), 12–14.

[366] CCC, 239–248, 253–255, 261–267; Wikipedia, "Trinity."

Christianity: Here are the primary arguments for and against the most significant religions and worldviews. Interestingly the debate comes down to the supernatural. The stronger the supernatural being, the greater the credibility. Similarly, the greater the miracles performed in the name of one's god or the other, the stronger the faith. It really comes down to measuring visible results in our physical world. In other words, the more a person can see, feel, touch, taste, hear with one's own senses, the greater the likelihood that person will begin to follow a particular religion or faith persuasion. This discussion is relevant to whether one even believes in a (G)od or not.

Let's match up the main religious worldviews and see which one comes out on top as being the true religion. The main arguments for each belief system and the Christian response are:

a. **Polytheists and Pagans**

Polytheism advocates present evidence that Polytheism is based on the worship of many gods including animistic sprits like animals and trees all the way to anthropomorphic gods which take on the appearance of man. These gods were collected in what we called pantheons. Their religion was referred to as mythology and polytheistic. Polytheists believe in many deities that are complex persons of greater and lesser status with differing skills, and with individual powers, abilities and knowledge. Gods of polytheism can be the highest part of a continuum that includes ancestors, demons, and spirits. Deities are often used to explain the observable and unobservable universe. Examples of the primary founded religions based on polytheism include: Taoism, Hinduism, Shintoism, Confucianism, Buddhism, and the tribal religions of

Africa and America.[367] Polytheists have many different complex beliefs, and some believe that their world is created organically and there is no creator god. Others believe in a creator deity. For example, Hindu Brahmans believe that Brahman created the universe and that there are secondary creators.[368] Hindus and Shintos believe in reincarnation rather than an eternal heaven with their creator. Polytheism is practiced by about 50% of today's world population.

The polytheism adherents will point out key differences between monotheism and polytheism. The key differences presented will be that monotheists believe the soul is greater than the body. Polytheists believe that the soul and body are equal. In monotheism, both philosophy and theology lead to revelation in the holy texts. Polytheists believe there is no theology, only mythology or epic poems, and holy texts consist of poems, songs, and ritual tradition. And monotheists look for individual personal connection and relationship with their god. In polytheism, there is no individual approach, but rather community is more important in rituals than the individual. Some traditions hold that one preserves his/her personality. Others say it is changed[369] Hindus believe that the world and life are an illusion, Maya, and not real.[370]

As for an afterlife, polytheists differ greatly in the concept. Some say the dead will be joined with their gods. Most traditions profess life after death and eternal life. Others profess

---

[367]Kowalcyak, Devin, "What's the Difference Between Polytheism and Monotheism," study.com, "Western Civilization 1"; and Id at "Polytheism: Definitions, Origins and Examples."

[368]Wikipedia, "Creator Deity."

[369]"Traditional Polytheist, Ten Differences Between Polytheism and Monotheism," www.traditionalpolythieist.com.

[370]Koukl, Greg, "Testing Religious Truth Claims, Stand to Reason" (www.str.org, February 20, 2013).

a reincarnation—either good or bad. Resurrection of the body varies by tradition, but the Egyptian and Zoroastrian are the most clear—under the dominion of a god. The concepts of judgment and justice vary by tradition. As for a savior, some polytheist traditions believe in a divine or semi-divine savior, i.e., an individual who will help the dead with merciful assistance, in terms of a future life. Not all traditions believe in eternal life for the world. Most traditions have some concept of a heaven or hell—reward or punishment for good or bad persons, respectively.[371]

Polytheists and pagans will claim miracles to prove their case but that evidence is nil. However, there are no proven miracles attributable to polytheism or paganism.

Christian Response and Rebuttal. In reply, The Christian response is that most of their gods are the handiwork of individuals, or even Satan, for selfish purposes. For example, the Hindu notion of Maya, that the world and life are merely an illusion, can be dismissed out of hand, as we all know this to be false. It is not a truthful statement. We do exist in a real world. And, if the fundamental premise to a polytheistic tradition is false, then it stands to reason that the remainder of claims and assertions as to the truth of the religion are also false, e.g., reincarnation. This also holds true for all of the polytheistic traditions.

There are no reliable proofs of the existence of any of these "gods." Most of them have been created by and rationalized to exist by humans. They have served certain needs of their believers over the centuries. However, there is no credible evidence that they actually exist.

In pantheism/polytheism, god and the universe are considered to be the same thing. In this view, the natural sciences are essentially studying the nature of god. This definition of god creates the

---

[371]Thomson, Gale, "Afterlife: An Overview" (www.encyclopedia.com, 2005).

philosophical problem that a universe with god and one without god are the same, other than the words used to describe it.[372] There is a rational disconnect here. One cannot hold to both premises. One or the other has to be true in their belief. And the unanswered question remains under their belief system—Who created the universe? That question is not answered. We know from incontrovertible scientific truths discussed above in this case, the universe was created by Creative Intelligent Design with extraordinary precision. Its creation was not happenstance.

"Deism and pantheism assert that there is a god distinct from, or which extends beyond (either in time or in space or in some other way) the universe. These positions deny that their god intervenes in the operation of the universe, including communicating with humans personally. The notion that God never intervenes or communicates with the universe, or may have evolved into the universe, makes it difficult, if not by definition impossible, to distinguish between a universe with a god and one without."[373] Instead, we know from scientific history, that a God has intervened constantly over the creation history of the universe and man. We have cogent and verifiable proof. We know from both scientific history and personal observations that God communicates regularly with humankind through His Angels and Saints, as discussed above. And we know, based on scientific, historical and scriptural proof that the Christian God loves each human so much that He gave up His only Son to come to earth, to suffer and die for our salvation, and later to be resurrected and ascended back in to Heaven. None of the pantheistic religions can rebut or disprove those Christian truths.

Pantheists/polytheists will make transcendental/logical arguments about the existence of a god. They will argue that human

---

[372]Wikipedia, "Existence of God."

[373]Id.

existence, experience, and action are sufficient to reason the existence of their gods, because a god is necessary to the creation of human intelligence. This is circuitous reasoning without a foundation. Who created their god, the universe, and matter? Where is their proof of the "uncaused first cause"? There is no logical extension of a proven foundation. Their gods cannot be rationally or logically proven. Much is left out in their reasoning process. Unlike the Christian proofs, their belief systems come down to pure belief and faith in their reasoning process. Where is their verifiable proof? They have no credible evidence of real miracles.

Miracles are variously defined as an event that is supernatural -violating the laws of nature, i.e., inexplicable, something is not normally observed, has religious significance and meaning and is performed at the hand of some transcendent rational agent or supernatural entity.[374] Of course, different cultures and religions may perceive a given event entirely differently, because of inherent biases. And miracles can be minor in nature or major. The concept of miracles is admittedly difficult to nail down with any precision. This is especially true in non-Christian settings.

Christians, on the other hand, contend and have proven that the many miracles performed by God, the Father, in the OT and by Jesus in the NT have not and could not be performed under the polytheistic and pagan traditions, simply because they have no supernatural god like our Judeo-Christian God. Further, Christians argue that those miracles claimed by the polytheists were mere wonders serving only the "miracle" performer, not the community or others, to strengthen belief in a Jewish or Christian God. Even St Augustine, great doctor of the Catholic Church, agreed that pagans could perform miracles, but those miracles were inferior to the power and scale of the Christian miracles. Satan can perform

---

[374]*The Cambridge Companion to Miracles*, Twelvetrees, Graham, Ed. (Cambridge University Press, 2011), 20 and 36.

"miracles" or "wonders." The apostles were in mortal combat with the polytheists and pagans. (Mark 6:7; Matt 10:1).[375] Further, the Christian Church asserts that a God and Savior, both divine and human, came to earth to be part of mankind, died for the human race and their sins, was resurrected from the dead by God, and ascended into Heaven. No polytheist or pagan can claim those miracles. None profess the miracles of the Christian faith observed after the death and resurrection of Jesus. This was the greatest recorded miracle in any religion in all of history. Finally, none of the polytheist traditions and miracles focuses on the theology of love of God and neighbor.

b. Monotheists.

Generally speaking, monotheists believe in a single God, who was creator and is immortal. As the Israelites moved out of Egypt in about 1375 BC, they adopted the first monotheistic religion we know as Judaism. God gave the new Jews the Ten Commandments to keep them on the straight and narrow. Other monotheistic beliefs have been created since then.

Judaism. Judaism is the first monotheistic religion created by God. Judaism is the foundation to the Christian faith. We believe in the same God. Christians are of the same Tree of Jesse as the Jews. Same God, but different theology on the Messiah, the Savior who opens the gates of Heaven for us. Many Jews are still waiting for the Messiah. Many now believe that Jesus, a Jew, is that savior. They are called Messianic Jews.

Christian Response. Christians assert that Jesus is the promised Messiah. Jesus is the fulfillment of the OT prophecies. The NT

---

[375]Id. at 82–90.

declares the message of salvation and of love. The Christian faith is the new true faith which God wishes us to pursue through the teachings of His Son, Jesus. The Law has been abolished, and the message of Love substituted in place. Jesus justified us to God the Father and we, as believers, are now responsible for our own sanctification, through the grace of salvation gifted to us by God. There is no more waiting for the Messiah. He has come. Jesus is our Savior and we must place our belief and faith in Him.

Mormonism. Although fundamentally monotheistic, as they worship only God the Father, Mormons also believe that they also have the power to attain the title of God and as children of God they also obtain His divine nature. In other words, people can become like gods in the afterlife.[376] Joseph Smith in 1820 had a vision from God claiming all the other Christian faiths had it wrong and that he was not to join. He was also given the golden tablets on which were inscribed the Book of Mormon, in an old Egyptian-type language. They believe in a form of the Trinity (Godhead), where God the Father, Son, and Holy Spirit are separate and distinctive persons—the Father and Son have human bodies and the Holy Spirit who is wholly spirit.

Most significantly Mormons believe that everyone is a child of God and that they can become divine just like Jesus Christ, who is considered a brother, i.e., joint heirs. They believe in an apostasy right after Jesus' ascension into Heaven. They believe the true Christian Church was restored by Joseph Smith and that Mormonism is the true Christian faith. Their cosmology incorporates the idea that everyone begins as a spirit in heaven with God and that everyone is free to accept or reject God's plan for salvation. The atonement of Jesus Christ is a central theme, and the purpose of an earthly existence is to discern between good and

---

[376]Wikipedia, Polytheism, Sec 8.2.1, Mormonism.

evil but that everyone can be saved through the atonement of Jesus. Everyone is expected to live a Christ-like life.[377]

Finally, Mormons do not believe in the Big Bang Theory of creation of the universe by God out of nothing. Instead, they believe God just reorganized existing matter. They contend that there are many other planets in the universe with life, the closest to God being the star/planet of Kolob (mentioned in the Book of Abraham, 1842).[378]

Christian Response—God's intervention. The immediate Christian Biblical response is that no one shall add to nor take away from the Ten Commandments (Deut 4:2; 12:32). If anyone who hears the word adds to them, they shall suffer plagues. If anyone takes away from the words the tree of life shall be removed from them (Rev 22:18–19). There are extensive scientific, philosophical, scriptural, and logical arguments proving the Mormon tradition is not based on Christianity and is fundamentally a cult—a religion of its own, not affiliated with mainstream beliefs, faiths or traditions. Mormonism contradicts the Bible. Christians can successfully rebut all of the Mormon contentions and assertions with the evidence presented herein. Christianity's primary argument is that Mormonism's foundational assertions and allegations have no substance in truth or fact in their foundation, and therefore all of the subsequent assertions fail. Their faith is limited to assertions in their books. There is no hard evidence—scientific, historical, philosophical, or scriptural (OT and NT) to back up their assertions. Their primary false assertion as to the nature and character of the Three Persons of the Trinity fail in light of the Christian hard evidence, argued and proven above. The Christian Church has proven over the millennia that God created the universe out

---

[377]Wikipedia, Mormonism

[378]Id.

of nothing. That God the Father, God the Son, and God the Holy Spirit are equal and are God. Humans cannot attain that level of holiness or godliness. We are subordinate and not equal to God. Even many atheists and agnostics believe that. Secondly, there is no scientific proof of a Kolob.

Further God is not human but rather a spirit. He is not married to a goddess. We are made in His image, not in His substance. Scripture, science, and nature prove this fact. There is no evidence of any recorded apostasy right after Jesus' ascension giving substance to their argument that Mormonism is the true Christian faith. Instead, we received the Holy Spirit, who is continually with us to protect us and to communicate between us and the Father and Son. The repeated references to Egyptology are also disconcerting in proving their case, as Moses brought God's people out of Egypt during the Exodus. If Egypt were the source of a reformed Egyptian language, it seems incongruous that this could have been the same OT and NT God.

The primary heresy of Mormonism as seen by Christians is the argument that a mortal human being can assume a divine nature like that possessed by the Trinity so that the individual rises to a state equal to that of Jesus and God. OT and NT scripture (God's proven Word) and its teachings, never make such a bold statement. There is no scriptural confirmation or proof that the Mormon statement of divinity is true. Joseph Smith was never confirmed in accepted OT or NT scripture, theology, or doctrine as a later-day apostle with the authority of God. If he were a true modern-day prophet, why do we not hear that message directly from God the Father or Jesus or the Holy Spirit? Finally, we see no miracles stemming from the Mormon Church. And the golden tablets have never been discovered or disclosed openly. Their existence is based on the world of Joseph Smith and not God. Again, if the foundational assertions of the Mormon Church are not sustainable or provable to the exclusion of the Christian Church, that faith and its traditions and practices are not credible nor proven and must be discounted as a mere cult.

Islam. Islam is an Abrahamic monotheistic religion with a single God (Allah). Muhammad is proclaimed to be his messenger. It is the second largest religion, with over 1.8 billion followers. Islam teaches that God is merciful, all-powerful, and unique. Muslims believe that it is a complete version of a primordial faith, revealed through Adam, Braham, Moses, and Jesus. The Quran is considered the unaltered and final revelation of God. Islam teaches that everyone is subject to judgment and reward in Heaven for the good and righteous, and eternal punishment in Hell for the bad and evil ones. The essence of this faith is the Five Pillars of Islam, requiring worship and following Sharia law. Islam was founded in the seventh century in the Middle East.

Doxology is based primarily on the concept of surrender or submission to the will of God. Their key theology is based on a single being, Allah. They do not believe in the Christian Trinity. They believe that God created everything—similar to the Big Bang Theory. The purpose of a Muslim is to worship and know their God. He is considered a personal God who will respond to requests for help. Muslims strongly believe in angels as spirit messengers who will deliver messages and revelations from God. Muslims believe that the Quran was dictated directly by God and was to replace the "distorted" Jewish Torah and Christian Gospel. They believe these verses were revealed to Muhammad by Angel Gabriel sometime between 610 and 632 AD. The Quran focuses on moral guidance and Islamic principles and values. Muslims identify prophets as those humans chosen by God. The prophets were to bring the "will of God" to the people. Prophets are human, but some can perform miracles to prove their significance. The primary message of Islam is submission to God. Muhammad was the last of the law-bearing prophets (including Jesus) who brought the final summarized word of God to the people. Traditions, known as hadiths, are meant to emulate Muhammad's actions. Muslims believe in a final judgment and bodily resurrection. Acts of worship are rendered under the Five Pillars of Islam. This includes testimony, prayer, charity, fasting, pilgrimage, Quranic recitation, and memorization.[379]

Islam is largely a theocratic existence. Day-to-day life is based on it. All government is based on it. Sharia law forms part of the religious tradition. It stems from the Quran and hadith. Jihad is a "struggle for God." A general jihad can be called by the leaders. A greater jihad can have a self-purification or perfection meaning. A lesser jihad can have a militaristic meaning—depends on the call.[380]

A miracle (mu'jizah) in the Quran is a supernatural intervention of Allah in the lives of ordinary human beings. Miracles confirm Allah's support of a particular prophet or messenger. They validate the truthfulness of their word.[381] Some minor miracles have been attributed to Muhammad as signs that he is a prophet—splitting of the moon in front of disbelievers, impossibly short time for trip between Mecca and Jerusalem, fed a thousand people out of his small dish without refilling multiple times, water flowed from a single small container in his hand in great volume, healing the sick, prayers immediately answered, tree trunk crying while Muhammad was teaching, and the Quran that God gave Muhammad.[382] Many of these miracles have been debunked as coincidences and not miracles (God's intervention) at all.[383] The Quran mentions many

---

[379] Wikipedia, "Islam."

[380] Id, at "Jihad."

[381] Anwaar, Amna, "Miracles in Islam," iQRA (www.islamicfinder.com, October 30, 2017).

[382] Ibraheem, Abu, "Miracles of Prophet Muhammad," (www.whyislam.org, March 30, 2015).

[383] WikiIslam, "Islam and Miracles."

miracles of Jesus and His apostles but not one for Muhammad.[384] And, interestingly, Muhammad was unable to perform miracles by his own admission. He did not claim to be a god but rather a warner (al-Ankabut 29:50). He claimed to be only the messenger (al-Isra 17:93).[385] The Quran itself indicates that Muhammad was incapable of miracles. The only possible "miracle" was the Quran. Many believers concede that any "miracles" were limited to those who perceived them.

The Quran makes many references to Jesus Christ and His miracles but treats him only as a great prophet. It also references Mary, the mother of Jesus, with great respect, as well as many angels.

Finally, and most significantly, the Quran explicitly disavows the crucifixion, death, burial, and resurrection of Jesus Christ. Islam believes that an imposter who looked like Jesus was crucified and that Jesus transcended bodily into Heaven.[386]

Christian response. Islam is an Abrahamic religion stemming from Ishmael, as Christianity stemmed from Isaac. Ishmael was the product of Sarah's handmaiden, Hagar (Gen 16:3). Isaac was born 14 years later to Sarah, when she was 90 years old (Gen 17:17 and 24). The Jewish God foretold that He would make his covenant with the people through Isaac (Gen 17:21). Isaac is the father of Judaism. Ishmael is the father of Islam, who would also be the founder of a great nation (Gen 17:20). However, Isaac's heritage

---

[384]Shamoum, Sam, "Muhammad and Miracles: Analyzing Muslim Arguments for Muhammad's Supernatural Feats," (www.answering-islam.org).

[385]St Mark Evangelist Association, "Miracles of the Living God" (www.3lotus.com).

[386]Quran, sura 4 (An-Nisa) ayat 157–158; Wikipedia, "Islamic Views on Jesus' Death."

was God's chosen track.[387] Verification is established through the scriptures and all the proofs set forth in this case. There is nothing in the Islam tradition that trumps the Christian tradition.

Miracles, properly discerned and proven, are one key to establishing and verifying the truth of God's divine support (John 10:38). The OT and NT miracles of God and Jesus respectively are absolutely proven beyond any reasonable doubt. Islam argues some miracles attributed to Muhammad; however, none have been proven as reliable. Some have been totally debunked. None rise to the level of reliability of the Jewish and Christian traditional miracles.[388] The Quran miracles claimed by Muslim scholars have no real basis in fact. Most claims are based on prophesies, coincidences, and interpretations, not supernatural events. They are not miracles in and of themselves.[389] Some believers claim that the Quran contains scientific knowledge that could not have been known 1,400 years ago.[390] However, again, many of these claims and prophecies do not equate to miracles or prophetic words in the traditional sense of the term. Instead they again equate to coincidences, without real or scientific evidence or proof.

The scientific-based miracles claimed by Islam are those proven to be created and sourced by the Christian God, e.g., creation, science, mathematics, geology, celestial objects, etc. They claim their God, Allah, to have been the source of these "miracles." Christians claim their Trinitarian God (Father, Son, and Holy Spirit) to be the source of miracle of creation and existence.

---

[387] Shamoun, Sam, "Abraham and Child of Sacrifice—Isaac or Ishmael?" (www.answering-islam.org).

[388] Hanegraaf, Hank, "Is Christianity the One True Religion?" One Place (www.oneplace.com).

[389] Wikipedia, "Quran and Miracles"; Ibrahim, Abu, 5 "Indisputable Miracles of the Quran," (Islamic Learning Materials, April 29, 2012).

[390] "Miracles of Quran," (www.miracles-of-quran.com).

Christianity also claims that one can come to know God the Father only through Jesus Christ, God the Son, who saved us from our sins. On the other hand, Islam rejects the Trinitarian concept of God, and holds that only Allah exists and that he has no son who reveals the truth of Allah. Islam, instead, teaches that Muhammad is the final and greatest prophet and messenger sent by God and claims Jesus was only a lesser prophet of his time. They do not believe Jesus was the Son of God or that he died for our sins.[391] Both faiths claim the supernatural power of their God. Only the Judaic/Christian God demonstrated His supernatural power many times through recorded miracles of Yahweh in the OT, e.g., Moses. Allah has not. Christians and Muslims do not worship the same God.[392] The Christian God is a personal God. God the Son died for our sins to save us. On the other hand, Allah is not a relational God.[393] Another key discerning factor to the truth between these two faiths is the supernatural power of the respective prophets, Islamic Muhammad (prophet) vs. Christian Jesus (God the Son). Based on reported and proven miracles noted above for both of these prophets, Jesus clearly displayed the supernatural power of miracles as God, but Muhammad, by his own admission, did not.

The Quran view on the crucifixion of Christ, is to deny He died on the cross for our sins but rather was taken bodily into Heaven by the Father belies the credibility and claim of Islam that it is the true religion. We know historically that the life, death on the cross, resurrection and ascension of Christ happened. It was to atone for the sins of man and reunite the human race with God the Father. Those events have been proven scripturally, philosophically, scientifically,

---

[391]"Islam vs. Christianity," All About Religion, (www.allaboutreligioin.org).

[392]Mohler, Albert, "Do Christians and Muslims Worship the Same God?" Billy Graham Evangelistic Association, (www.billygraham.org, December 1, 2013).

[393]Janosick, Daniel, *Is Allah of Islam the same as Yaweh of Christianity?* Columbia International University (www.ciu.edu).

and historically (see above). Although they may appear similar on the surface, these religions are diametrically opposed in core doctrinal doxology—the way of salvation. The logical extension is that Islam is not the true faith. Rather, Christianity is.

Finally, the logical extension from the Quran itself leads to the following conclusion:

Islam teaches that the Quran is the absolute truth revealed from their god Allah. It further states, and this is critical, that if one fact in the Quran is incorrect, then Islam is not true. But the Quran teaches a man's seed comes from his chest, not testes (Quran 86:5–7). It describes crucifixion before its invention (Quran 7:123–124) and says that birds and ants can talk (27:16; 27:18). Since these are not true, Islam can't be either.[394]

Again, the hard evidence proves Christianity to be the one and only true faith established by God.

C. Summary of Christian Arguments Rebutting Polytheism and Other Monotheistic Beliefs

Jesus said, "I am the way, the truth, and the life, and no one comes to the Father but by me" (John 14:6). "For God so loved the world, that He gave His only begotten Son, that whoever believes in Him shall not perish, but have eternal life" (John 3:16). "Whoever believes in the Son has eternal life" (John 3:36). These and all of the scriptures of the OT and NT are God inspired. How could the prophets of old been able to discern the relative order of the creation of the earth by a creator? The prophesies as to the coming of the Messiah? Logic dictates that they were inspired by a God Creator. By a God who loves us and wants the best for us.

---

[394] Slick, Matt, "How Do We Know that Christianity is True and That we are not Deceived?" Christian Apologetics and Research Ministry (CARM) (www.carm.org, December 12, 2008).

Otherwise why would He have sent His Son to suffer and die for our sins?

Christianity is the only religion that has God the Creator reaching down to us and leading us to salvation and eternal life through His Son, Jesus Christ. Jesus did it all for us. He justified each of His followers to God the Father. He did all the work. All we need to do is to keep our souls pure and serve God and others. The basis of Christianity is love of God and one another. All the other religions instead, have their faithful followers doing some act for God to earn salvation. There is no emphasis on love in the pantheistic/polytheistic religions or even in the other monotheistic religions. Their god's all demand some sort of performance—earning one's way to Heaven. And all of the pantheistic/polytheistic religions have different concepts of life after—typically without an eternal heaven.

The only possible common denominator to discern the truth between these religions is the concept of proven power of a "God" through supernatural miracles. As argued above, most religions have not demonstrated actual performed miracles. Islam has claimed some but Muhammad has expressly debunked them. Judaism has demonstrated miracles with Abraham, Moses, and some of the other prophets, but those miracles ceased with the advent of Christianity 2,000 years ago. Jesus and His Apostles have demonstrated their supernatural spiritual powers through miracles many times in the NT and up to the present. These miracles demonstrate the power of the one and only true God. Therefore, on the basis of performance of physical and spiritual miracles alone, Christianity has demonstrated overwhelmingly it is the true faith. Those miracles are discussed in detail above.

Truth is a function of authority, credibility, and reliability. None of the polytheistic or other non-Judeo-Christian monotheistic religions are credible, trustworthy, reliable, or verifiable. So far, only Christianity presents a verifiable option, proven in science, philosophy, metaphysics, OT and NT Biblical scripture, and historic documents (both Christian and non-Christian).

Christianity is able to definitively rebut, beyond any reasonable doubt, each claim of polytheism and monotheism (non-Christian) that they are the only true religion! Only Christianity can lay legitimate claim to being the one and only true religion and faith. Therefore, the substantive Divine Law as defined in the Christian Bible (OT and NT) is the true faith that will lead you to the truth of the existence of the only true God for you to believe in.

Even though we can prove the existence of God, only you can step up in faith to believe in that God. The evidence is there. Only you can choose to believe or not. I pray you make the correct decision. Your eternal life depends on it!

2. There is no scientific proof of God. To the contrary there is extensive scientific and physical evidence and proof of God (see my answer to question 1 above). One need only look around at the intricately designed living environment on planet earth and the expanses of the physical universe. These manifestations are proof of the existence of a God:

Big Bang Theory. First, almost all scientists, religious and non-religious, agree on the concept of the Big Bang as the creation of mass and energy as the core constituents of the physical universe we experience and live in. 60% of scientists believe in a God![395] This fact alone is a great testament to the proof of a living and loving God. However, for the religious and theological skeptics, Creation of the universe under the Big Bang Theory had to be by a supernatural force. It was planned and designed by God. There is no other logical explanation.

---

[395] Spitzer, Fr Robert, "Essential 2: Proof of God's Existence," Credible Catholic (Magis Center), www.crediblecatholic.com, 2017) slide 11.

To this point, Paul the later Apostle, perceived and prophesied the eventual revelation of creation:

Since what may be known about God is plain to them, because God has made it plain to them. For since the creation of the world God's invisible qualities—his eternal power and divine nature—have been clearly seen, being understood from what has been made, so that people are without excuse (Romans 1:19–21).

See the discussion above in the previous topic for more detailed explanation of the science proving the existence of a God, Designer, and Creator. There is no other logical or reasoned explanation for the cause of this phenomenon other all-powerful, all-knowing, and purposeful Intelligent Designer—God!

When we look at the physical universe, most of us do not take that reality for granted. We question its creation. Was there a supernatural being that pulled the stuff of the universe together? Did it just come into being from nothing? Where did all the mass and energy come from? Out of nothing? How could that be as that would violate certain laws of thermodynamics.[396] Our limited human understanding of the physical universe leads to many hypotheses and suggestions. However, if God created all energy and matter and was the "cause" of the Big Bang, as most Christians now believe spiritually, He certainly could have created all of the laws of physics, thermodynamics, electromagnetics, and mathematics as well as all the other sciences simultaneously, that regulate the properties of that energy and matter.

Immutable Rules of Thermodynamics: 1) energy can neither be created nor destroyed. It is conserved in one form or another, and 2) Law of entropy, i.e., energy is dissipating and not being created. It can only change form or be transferred from one object to another. Every energy transfer that takes

---

[396] "The Laws of Thermodynamics, First and Second Laws of Thermodynamics as they apply to Biological Systems," Khan Academy (www.khanacademy.org, 2015).

place will increase the entropy of the universe and reduce the amount of usable energy available to do work (or, in the most extreme case, leave the overall entropy unchanged). All forms of energy can eventually be converted to heat and can be dissipated throughout the universe. Temperatures over an extensive period of time will eventually even out, creating a randomness. That energy will be lost to randomness. The degree of randomness is called entropy.

One can rationally reason, therefore, that mass and energy had to be intelligently imagined and created. Although energy may experience entropy toward a balanced random universe, the creation of mass and energy at the Big Bang was not a random event. These rules of thermodynamics are founded by God in His Natural Laws—laws that govern the universe and everything in it.

Universal Constants—Examples: 1) speed of light, 2) Newtonian constant of gravity, 3) Planck constant, and 4) reduced Planck constant.[397]

Electromagnetic Constants: 1) magnetic constant, 2) electric constant, 3) characteristic impedance in a vacuum, 4) Coulomb's constant, 5) elementary charge, 6) Bohr magneton, 7) conductance quantum, 8) inverse conductance quanta, 9) Josephson constant, 10) magnetic flux quantum, 11) nuclear magneton, and 12) von Klitzing constant.

Atomic and Nuclear Constants: 1) Bohr radius, 2) classical electron radius, 3) electron mass, 4) Fermi coupling constant, 5) fine-structure constant, 6) Hartree energy, 7) proton mass, 8) quantum of circulation, 9) Rydberg constant, 10) Thomson cross section, and 11) weak mixing angle.

Physico-chemical Constants: 1) atomic mass constant, 2) Avogadro constant, 3) Boltzman constant, 4) Faraday constant, 5) first radiation constant, 6) Loschmidt constant, 7) gas constant, 8)

---

[397]Wikipedia, "Physical Constant."

molar Planck constant, 9) molar value of an ideal gas, 10) Sackur-Tetrode constant, 11) second radiation constant, 12) Stefan-Boltzmann constant, 13) Wien displacement law constant, and 14) Wien-Bonal entropy displacement constant.[398]

Other constants on a more universal scale include:

> Placement of objects in space: mass and energy (black holes) and smaller bodies in orbit around larger bodies in equilibrium, are not products of random acts of nature. They were also intelligently planed and implemented.
>
> Perfect Alignment of Planetary Objects: Also consider the odds of a perfect eclipse of the sun by the moon, with a slight penumbra. Divide the sun's diameter (864,576 miles) by the moon's (2,159) = 400.52. The distance of the earth from the sun (93,000,000 mile) by the distance of the moon from the earth 239,000 miles) = 389.121.[399] Odds are $1/10^{50}$ that the planets would randomly align perfectly and maintain their orbits.[400]
>
> Physical Constants Gravitational Constant – Fine Tuning: There are many other rules of physics at work in the universe between objects—both visible and invisible. Many of these rules of physics involve gravitational attraction

---

[398] Id.

[399] Metaxas, Eric, "Are Solar Eclipses Proof of God?" (Fox News, August 20, 2017); Asec, "The Solar Eclipse is Against the Odds in ANY Solar System, Evidence to Consider" (December 1, 2012).

[400] Spitzer, Fr Robert, "Essential 2: Proof of God's Existence," Credible Catholic (Magis Center, www.crediblecatholic.com), slide 44.

between objects and within the atomic and molecular structure of elements themselves.

As noted above, British Cosmologist and astrophysicist, Martin John Rees, president of the Royal Society (2005–10) pinpointed six major physical constants enabling the universe and our planet to function. The first two relate to basic forces; the second two fix the size and texture of the universe and determine whether it will live forever; the last two fix the properties of space:[401]

Physical Earth. Finally, let's look at our physical surroundings here on earth. Earth orbits the sun in a "zone of life." This means that the earth is perfectly positioned at 193 million miles from the sun. Temperatures are such that earth can maintain oceans and an atmosphere. We have the essential elements of C, H, and O required for organic life.

Now, again to the question at hand. Do you believe that God, the Father is the planner, designer, and creator of the universe? Or do you believe in another theory of creationism without God? if so, does your theory of creation correlate with rational reality? Is there scientific proof supporting your theory or god? Does it weather the challenge of reason and logic? Does it withstand legitimate spiritual challenge? What (G)od do you believe in? Is he/she/it an eternal omnipotent supernatural (G)od capable of creating the universe and each of us, with absolute balance and perfection? Is the basic physical proof laid out above not sufficient to convince you that there is but one supreme God capable of accomplishing all of creation purely out of love for each of us. He did this with one goal in mind—our salvation and eternal life for each of us with Him in the spiritual universe which we shall unquestionably experience after we die and leave this physical universe. Again, we

---

[401] Rees, Martin, Just Six Numbers: The Deep Forces That Shape the Universe, Chapter 1: The Cosmos and the Microworld (Basic Books, 2000), p 2.

have free choice to accept a belief in this God, the Father and His Son, Jesus Christ who died on the cross for us to reconcile us back to God after the fall of Adam and Eve with Original Sin. What is your choice? Can you accept the free grace and love of God? You have the opportunity to accept Him and His Son, Jesus Christ and be baptized. You have the opportunity to repent and confess your sins after baptism. You have the opportunity to live a life of love for God and for neighbor. Your salvation and eternal with God are that simple!

I believe firmly that those who do not believe in the Christian God, or His Son, Jesus Christ, will face a terrible judgment before Jesus at both the initial and final judgments! Therefore, the reason for this book! I pray that each of us is judged favorably, and will spend eternity in loving peace and joy with the Holy Trinity. The alternative is unbelievably hopeless and harsh—physical pain and separation from God, the Father, our loving creator, God the Son, Jesus Christ, our savior, and God the Holy Spirit. We will also have no contact with loved ones, family and friends. Just pure torture and suffering in Hell at the hand of Satan! The choice to believe in God the Father and God the Son, is yours! Please choose wisely!

3. Science, common sense and reason give me all the answers and are incompatible with religion and I can learn all I need to know about God and creation on my own without religion.

Oh really? I disagree. Let's explore this line of reasoning.

First, The concept and theology of a (G)god has been studied by humankind continuously since 10,000 BC.[402] Most religious beliefs for which there is documented history reach back to about 5,000 BC.[403] Judaism roots reach back to 2,000 BC with Abraham (founding father of the covenant with God) although Moses

---

[402]Wikipedia, "Timeline of Religion."

[403]Id.

(author of the first five books of the bible—Pentateuch or Torah) is considered the father of the Jewish faith with the advent of the Ten Commandments from God about 1,450 BC. Interestingly the Egyptians were developing their own beliefs about the same time.[404] Minoan polytheistic rituals reach back to 2,200 BC. Hinduism found its roots about 1,600 BC. Confucianism developed around 600 BC and Buddhism about 500 BC.[405]

My point is that religion has been around for many millennia in many forms. Many authors and theologians have attempted to explain religion over thousands of years. It always has been a topic of great interest and coverage. Religion and the existence of God have been studied to great depths. And still the theologians and religious writers cannot agree on what the truth of God is. An individual who believes they can discern the truth on their own by spontaneous revelation will be sadly mistaken. Many believing they had the truth came to their own unfounded isolated conclusions. Many sects of the Christian faith have developed. For instance, there are over 40,000 different sects of Christian Protestantism. Now, many of the points of disagreement may be relatively minor, procedural and inconsequential; however, the point is that one cannot tackle the question of God's existence in a vacuum or without extensive reading, discussion, debate, and prayer. It is through "iron sharpening iron" we come to the truth. I believe God welcomes the debate. It gives Him an open mind to weigh in with his truth. But to say that divine revelation will come to someone without the prerequisite of hard work, study and reflection, and most importantly, prayer, is irrational and folly. It won't happen. Everyone needs to engage on the issue. Personal engagement is necessary. That is not to say, however, that God may not make Himself obvious to someone at any time. He is God

---

[404] Id.

[405] Id.

and He can act according to His will. But the risk of sitting back and waiting for God to reveal Himself could be spiritually disastrous. I was not willing to take that chance of passing up the offer of Jesus for eternal salvation, which required my individual acceptance and action.

Second, as for science, as we learned above, science and religion are not incompatible but rather totally consistent. Science (scientific proof and reason) does not hold all the answers. Religion (faith and belief based in science, historicity, and spirituality) does not hold all the answers. God intended the heart and mind work together to lead us to the ultimate truth of His existence and His love for each of us. Makes sense because God created both areas in our beings to study and reflect on the word of God. Each is able to help explain the other. Together, they will lead you to the truth, faith and belief in the true God.

Third, today, many of America's youth have developed an overconfidence and feeling of independence and self-empowerment through relativism, materialism, secularism and scientism. In other words, they feel they can figure things out for themselves. They have all the answers. There is a modern-day feeling that there is no need to refer to old standards, concepts, beliefs, traditions, doctrines, etc. We see it in those pursuing a Bohemian lifestyle, disconnected from the structure and stricture of society. A "go it alone" mind-set. Individualism is defined "as the moral stance, political philosophy, ideology, or social outlook that emphasizes the moral worth of the individual. Individualists promote the exercise of one's goals and desires and so value independence and self-reliance and, therefore, advocate that interests of the individual should achieve precedence over the state or a social group, while opposing external interference upon one's own interests by society or institutions such as the government."[406]

---

[406] Wikipedia, "Individualism."

God has made Himself obvious as scripture tells us We just need to look around. But God reveals Himself best through His Church. Scholars have been down this theological path many times. We don't need to reinvent the proverbial wheel. We just need to tap into the writings of our spiritual forefathers and their prophesies and proclamations to discern the real truth about God. Seeking God in an individualistic vacuum will lead nowhere, unless He miraculously reveals Himself through interlocutions—very rare indeed. God wants us to work out our individual salvation by seeking Him out. He wants us to peel the religious and scientific onions. He wants us to educate ourselves through study, contemplation, and prayer. He has sent the Holy Spirit to help us in this task. But we must ask. Remember, God will never force Himself on us, but He will give us the grace to know Him and each person of the Holy Trinity. One need only search Him out. He is there to help. I suggest the sincere seeker of truth start with Holy Scripture and in the Catholic tradition, the Catechism. All the answers lie within these two sources of the truth about God. We also need to pray and study the many books and articles written about God and the Christian faith to develop an understanding of the true faith. We are fortunate that the heavy spiritual lifting has already been done by our forefathers. There are many excellent resources available. We rest spiritually on their shoulders. God will continue to reveal the truth of Himself, salvation, and eternal life to us through these sources. Just like peeling the spiritual onion, one layer at a time.

I am always concerned when someone says he/she can figure God out on his/her own. That is like saying, I can figure out how to be a brain surgeon, nurse, lawyer, or engineer on my own. I don't need any training, schooling, or study. This is self-centered, egotistical, arrogant, and erroneous and dangerous thinking. None of us was designed to live in a vacuum. We were each created with specific skill sets and abilities. Have you considered the realities of vocations and professions? Isn't it amazing that each of us is wired differently to fill certain occupational niches? Does it make sense that all youth have been given the inspiration to figure out these nuances of theology and science on their own? I don't think so. That is a high numerical improbability. We were created uniquely as individuals by God to interact with Him and each other with love. No two of us humans are created exactly the same—physically, mentally, or spiritually. This is God's plan. We are dependent on one another. We are to share and learn from each other. Google is about the only "AI," with its complex algorithms that can tout having nearly all of mankind's knowledge and learning at hand. Remember, it is individuals who share their knowledge and input into Google. There are billions of books and articles written each year by individuals with distinct talents and knowledge. And programmers create the extreme algorithms, and research and contributions to this central source of info. None of us individually can do this. You might well say that Google and other search engines are your source of info where you will learn about God. I say, right on. I do much of my research into theology, philosophy, and science online myself. It is an efficient and comprehensive source of knowledge and information. However, I constantly update myself with current events to capture current thinking of the scholars, theologians, denominations, other faiths, religions, and worldviews continually as I write more books. However, I also interact with clergy, fellow Christians, those of other faith persuasions to place all of this into proper perspective, to continually develop myself spiritually and improve my own knowledge and understanding of God. I learn from each of them. However, most importantly, I spend time in prayer and internal reflection to get to know God better. I find that I have to use all these sources, to make certain my work is as accurate as possible. My research is a wonderful adventure as I come closer to God. This is what He wants—for each of us to search Him out, to compare Him with other gods. Trust me, He is not afraid of the competition for our hearts and minds. Compare Him as Creator and His Son, Jesus Christ as our Savior, and the Holy Spirit, as Jesus' continuing presence in our lives on this earth, and communicator, all together as the Christian Holy Trinity, with the thousands of other spiritual choices available in this world. You can readily reference the proofs of the Christian God in the chapters above. Consider the overwhelming evidence of the existence of this Christian God, compared to other (G)ods. Consider the supernatural nature and power or this God, the extensive miracles performed by God the Father and Jesus, the Son, and continuing miracles after His death and resurrection. No other monotheistic or polytheistic (G)od can claim these supernatural powers. For the atheist, agnostic or non-believer, this should be sufficient evidence to prove the Christian God is The true God! But you must decide the objective truth for yourself!

Through an active comparative theology approach, one can discern who/what makes most sense in the spiritual sense. My point is that the complexity of one's spiritual beliefs cannot be meaningfully or intelligently developed without study, reflection, and human intellectual and spiritual interaction. Even if you claim to be an atheist, you must know what you do not believe in. Same for the agnostic who believes in a superior being and power but not necessarily a particular god.

Summing up, I believe it is very dangerous to try to develop one's concept of a (G)od, or conversely, the non-existence of God, on one's own in an intellectual and spiritual vacuum. The spiritual explorer must study, reflect, and interact with others to discern the true God. You cannot do this on your own. You must engage and discuss. The consequences are significant and eternal. It is important that you get this process correct. There is no stepping back and reconfiguring your beliefs once you die. You are stuck with those developed beliefs when you leave the earth. You have to get this right! It is important you discern the spiritual truth.

God will not interfere with your beliefs, but He will give you the grace to know Him if you ask. In my first book, *You, Me and God: A Reflection on Intimate Relationships*, I recounted my formal YWAM training into knowing God and sharing Him with others. I share the truths of the existence of God (the Holy Trinity) I learned during that period of intense study and interactive training. I sought Him out, in sincerity, and He showered me with the grace to know Him better. I am now sharing Him with others. I commend such a program to each of my readers. Give the Christian God a chance in your life. Seek Him out with a sincere heart. Study all religions, faiths, and spiritual worldviews. Study Christianity and the Christian God. Seek out the truth about your creator, eternal life with Him after death. Get to know Him. Ask Him for favor and help in every aspect of your life. Compare this God with other gods—monotheistic and polytheistic. Learn about Him. Importantly, talk to others about Him. See what they say. Discuss and debate Him. God loves to see this interaction. Get to know Him. Please, do your spiritual homework. Then make your decision. That is all God asks of you.

4. I don't like formalized and hierarchical religion and religious leaders. I understand and sometimes share the frustrations of religious hierarchy and church leadership within the Christian Church. Especially today, we have many issues within formalized religion. For example, at the time of this writing, the Catholic Church is suffering through the reeling effects of sexual abuse scandal of many priests over the last 50 years. Investigation continues on who in the hierarchy knew about these despicable abuses and what was done to stop them. This is truly a sad time in the Church. All Catholics are disgusted with not only the abuses but more significantly with the cover-up over many years. Absolutely inexcusable! However, we have also seen many sexual scandals and adulterous affairs within the Protestant denominations. A number of televangelists come to mind. I have seen or heard of embezzlements, heretical teachings, etc. Both spiritual and secular failings and sin have crept into every church at one time or another. Christianity is not immune. Church leaders are human, not divine, and subject to temptation. We all fall short of the glory of God!

However, the failings within the formalized and hierarchical Christian Church and within some of the leadership are not a failure of God, or even of the church as the "bride of Christ," but rather the failure of imperfect humans entrusted with the keys to God's Church. God does not interfere in our lives. He has given us free will. He will not interfere with free will and stop sin. That would be incongruous with granting us each free will. God is not a God of conflicts—His will is perfect and not embedded with contradictions. This is true even within the hierarchy of the Church. Unfortunately, God ends up wittingly or unwittingly with most of the blame and a spiritual "black eye" because of what His church leaders have done. Some argue that the blame should go partially to Him "because, He could have done something." At times, God will interfere. Examples include saving clergy from deadly attacks, preservation of a church threatened by flood, fire, destruction, miracles to prove His existence. But not always. Only God knows his motivation. Often, however, He allows suffering, death, and destruction at the hands of humans or nature, to deepen our dependence on Him, to build spiritual character, or for other reasons we cannot fathom. God is God, and He does what he pleases, whether we agree or not. His ways are far above our ways. He sees the entire picture, past, present, and future. We can only see the past and present. God's will is many times unsearchable. But we know that His purpose is to prosper us and not harm us, as we are His creation and His children. We cannot blame God for the human failings of others or for suffering or even death. He does not cause these things, but He may allow them for reasons of His own, that we may never understand until we join Him in eternity.

Now, having shared the human side of the hierarchy of the Christian Church and its admitted human shortcomings, the spiritual side of the hierarchy, as inspired by God, is still perfect as the will of God is perfect. It is up to each of us individually to discern the difference and always seek out spiritual truths of the love of God and His plan for our salvation. Sometimes that discernment process gets clouded, but we must continue to try.

So why do we need hierarchy within a church? Precisely for the reasons noted above. There are good reasons for a hierarchy within many of the mainstream Christian churches. One primary purpose is to preserve true doctrine and teachings of the Church from human schisms. Human error can wittingly or unwittingly derail spiritual truth. We call these errors or failures heresies. The effort of the Christian Church should always be to discern God's truths—they should always lead us to salvation and eternal life with Him.

The Catholic Church magisterium has dealt with heresies over the 2,000 years of its existence. It has held a number of councils to deal with many heresies and attacks on the faith and to preserve the true traditions of the Christian Church. For nearly 2,000 years the Catholic Church has been the single repository of scriptural teachings in both the Old and New Testaments. The scholars and theologians of the church have helped preserve and explain the truth of the scriptures and doctrines of our faith preserved through oral and written tradition. The Catholic repository is now contained within sacred scripture (73 books) and sacred tradition, which is called the Catechism of the Catholic Church (CCC). As Catholic Christians we believe both these to be the inspired word of God, handed down to us to help us in our earthly journey through life, and to prepare us for eternity. Protestants believe that sacred scripture contains 66 books of the Bible, inspired by God. They profess belief in the literal word of Scripture—"Sole Scriptura." They commonly reject the Pope and Catholic Catechism as being heretical. They do not accept the traditions of the Catholic church, aka Catechism of the Catholic Church.

The good news is that whether Catholic Christian or Protestant Christian or Orthodox Christian, we still have much in common—belief in the Trinity and God Head, Jesus Christ as savior, repentance and forgiveness of sin and salvation through belief in Jesus, repentance of sin after Baptism, and leading sanctified and holy lives, loving God and neighbor all leading to eternal life with God in Heaven. This is the God-inspired side of our faith and beliefs. This is what propels us into His waiting arms for eternity. We need only accept Him, believe in His Son, Jesus Christ repent of our sins, and lead good lives. These beliefs are held in common by the Catholic Church, Orthodox Church, and more mainstream conservative Protestant Churches. This is the key to the repository of our faith that is maintained by the Christian Church hierarchy.

The truth of the Christian God and the faith are deposited and maintained within the structure, organization, repository, and hierarchy of this church. Otherwise faith would be random, determined by individuals (individualism) without inspiration from God. Many would be false teachings and would not gain us eternal life with God. The whole purpose of a church is to gain salvation and eternal life for each of our souls. We could not do this without a church hierarchy protecting the sacred truths and doxology of the Christian faith. The message of salvation must be singular and unified. It must be protected from heresy. It must be preserved. That is the function of the Christian Church hierarchy.

Another purpose is organization and unity of spiritual belief. Without centralized organization and hierarchy, the Christian church would be splintered and going in many different directions. Take for example, the Protestant Church with its 40,000 different denominations. Although there are certain core Christian beliefs common to most of these denominations, there are still many philosophical and theological differences. This posture creates a fractured picture of the Godhead, salvation, methods of worship and life eternal. This spiritual discord causes a split within the body of Christ. Protestants unwilling to work with Catholics toward common goals and vice versa. This is not God's will. He wants a unified Church. Fortunately, the Catholic and Lutheran leadership have been working together for over 10 years to bridge the chasm of Christian spirituality. I am hopeful and prayerful these efforts bear fruit in the future.

Two key examples of diverse spiritual beliefs within the Christian church are the rapture and millennialism. Catholics are amillennial, meaning they believe we are in final times since the Pentecost and that there will be no rapture of Christians prior to the second coming of Jesus. Protestants, depending on their denomination, are largely split between pre-tribulation millennialism and post-tribulation millennialism, resulting in discord and confusion. This is a spiritual difference. Some say serious, others say minor. Whatever, one's individual take or belief, we all have to agree that God does not promote confusion. He is a God of spiritual unity and clarity. So what is God's inspired word on this matter?

Let's explore the different concepts of post- and pre-tribulation and millennialism:

Post-Tribulation—Conservative Protestants. Post-tribulation rapture doctrine holds that there is a resurrection of dead believers and rapture or translation (or a taking-up/catching-away) of living believers in Jesus Christ at the end of the age (or the "end time"). Post-tribulationists believe that Christians will remain on the Earth throughout a whole seven-year tribulation period which includes the last three and a half years, which some differentiate by calling the last three and a half years the Great Tribulation period. The main and distinguishing feature of post-tribulationalism is that it holds that the rapture will occur after a seven-year tribulation period and not before it as in pre-tribulationism or after three and a half years as in mid-tribulationalism tribulation period and not before it as in pre-tribulationism or after three and a half years as in mid-tribulationalism.[407]

New Testament support for post-tribulation is found in Matthew 24:29–31 and 1 Thesselonians. 4:15–17. See also the parallel passages from Mark 13:24–27 and Luke 21:20–28.

Pre-tribulation—Progressive Evangelical Protestants: Pre-tribulation rapture theology originated in the eighteenth century, with the Puritan preachers Increase Mather (1639–1723) and Cotton Mather (1663–1728), and was popularized extensively in the 1830s by John Nelson Darby (1800–1882) They held to the idea that believers would be caught up in the air, followed by judgments on earth, and then the millennium.[408]

Pre-tribulationists believe that all Christians then alive will be taken bodily up to Heaven (called the rapture) before the tribulation begins. They often quote 2 Thessalonians 2:6–7 to support the idea that the Holy Spirit will be withdrawn as a stabilizing influence on secular society (Matt 5:13) through the removal of the Church. Those who become converts after the rapture will, like the Old Testament saints, not be indwelt by the Holy Spirit in the same sense as Christians are said to be today. They will live through (or perish during) the tribulation. After the tribulation, Christ will return. This relatively new doctrine has become the most widely accepted eschatological doctrine in the United States during the past century. It is commonly taught in the vast majority of evangelical churches to the exclusion of all others.[409]

---

[407]Wikipedia, "Post-Tribulation Rapture."

[408]Wikipedia, "Rapture."

[409]Wikipedia, "Post-tribulation," supra.

Scriptural support for pre-tribulationism is found in the Book of Revelation 20:1–6. Pre-tribulation support is also found in Matthew 24:37-40. The pre-tribulation rapture was popularized in Tim LaHaye *Left Behind* series.[410]

Amillennialism—Catholics and Conservative Protestants: In the amillennial and postmillennial views there are no distinctions in the timing of the rapture. These views regard the rapture as it is described in 1 Thess. 4:15-17—it would be identical to the second coming of Jesus as described in Matt 24:29–31 after an actual (post millennialism) or symbolic millennium (amellenialism).[411] Post-tribulationists perceive the rapture as occurring simultaneously with the second coming of Christ. Upon Jesus' return, believers will meet him in the air and will then accompany him in his return to the Earth.[412] The amillennialist view (no specific period of time) is the position held by the Roman Catholic, Eastern Orthodox, and Anglican churches, as well as mainline Protestant bodies, such as Lutherans, Methodists, Presbyterians, and many Reformed congregations.[413]

Amillennialism emphasizes New Testament passages that call the time immediately following the resurrection of Christ the "last days." To the amillennialist, this means that the millennium began with Christ and although the phrase "last days" seemingly conveys a short period of time, it apparently means more than 2,000 years

---

[410]Wikipedia, "Rapture," supra

[411]Id.

[412]Id.

[413]Id.

since Christ has not yet returned. The amillennialist suggests the phrase refers to the final era of history.[414]

Catholics do not believe in rapture or that the 1,000 years is literal, but instead symbolic and believe that we have been in the "End Times" or "Last Days" for the last 2,000 years since the incarnation of Jesus.[415] An important passage to the amillennialist is Acts 2:17–21. In this passage, Peter addresses a crowd and quotes the Old Testament prophet, Joel. The passage reads:

> "Thus you will know that I am in the midst of Israel, and that I am the Lord your God, And there is no other; And My people will never be put to shame.

The Promise of the Spirit" It will come about after this That I will pour out My Spirit on all mankind; And your sons and daughters will prophesy, Your old men will dream dreams, Your young men will see visions. Even on the male and female servants I will pour out My Spirit in those days.

The Day of the Lord I will display wonders in the sky and on the earth, Blood, fire and columns of smoke. The sun will be turned into darkness And the moon into blood Before the great and awesome day of the Lord comes. And it will come about that whoever calls on the name of the Lord Will be delivered; For on Mount Zion and in Jerusalem There will be those who escape, As the Lord has said, Even among the survivors whom the Lord calls. (Joel 2:27:32; NASB)

---

[414]"Amillennialism, Religion Facts" (www.religionfacts.com, March 13, 2013 and updated October 29, 2016).

[415]Olson, Carl E, "Eschatological Fact and Fiction: Catholicism and Dispensationalism Compared" (Ignatius Insight, June 10, 2006).

The larger context of this passage is the coming of the Holy Spirit, which occurred shortly after Christ's resurrection and ascension. Peter calls this time the "last days" by means of quoting the Old Testament prophet Joel. Therefore, to the amillennialist, the world has been in an eschatological stage since the time of Christ. Amillennialists also believe that Revelation 20:1–6 is a glimpse and description of this current stage.[416] Interestingly, note that Revelation 20:1–6 is also cited by the Pre-trib Mellennialists in support of their spiritual position.

Amillennialists also cite Hebrews 1:1–2 in their argument:

> God, after He spoke long ago to the fathers in the prophets in many portions and in many ways, ² in these last days has spoken to us in His Son, whom He appointed heir of all things, through whom also He made the world. Heb 1:1-2 (NASB)

Support is also found in Paul's writings to the Thessalonians (1 Thess. 4:15–17; NASB):

> For this we say to you by the word of the Lord, that we who are alive and remain until the coming of the Lord, will not precede those who have fallen asleep. ¹⁶ For the Lord Himself will descend from heaven with a shout, with the voice of *the* archangel and with the trumpet of God, and the dead in Christ will rise first. ¹⁷ Then we who are alive and remain will be caught up together with them in the clouds to meet the Lord in the air, and so we shall always be with the Lord.

---

[416] Id.

GOD, ARE YOU FOR REAL?

Summary: The following are two charts putting the above concepts into a graphic picture to help understand the concepts of pre and post-tribulation as distinguished from the concept of millennialism:

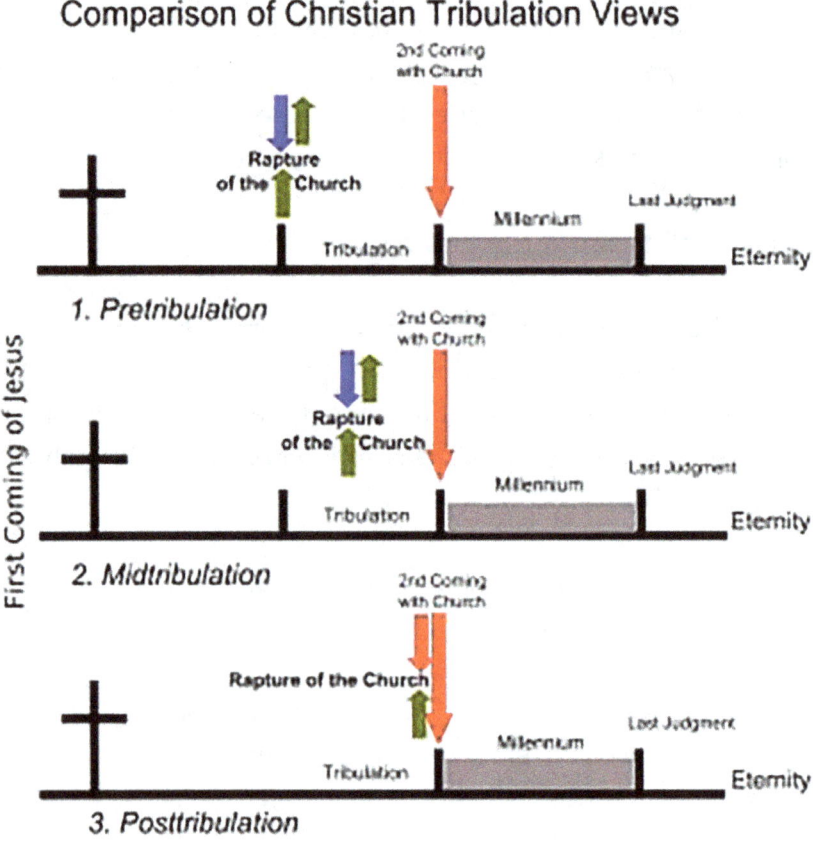

417

---

[417] Id.

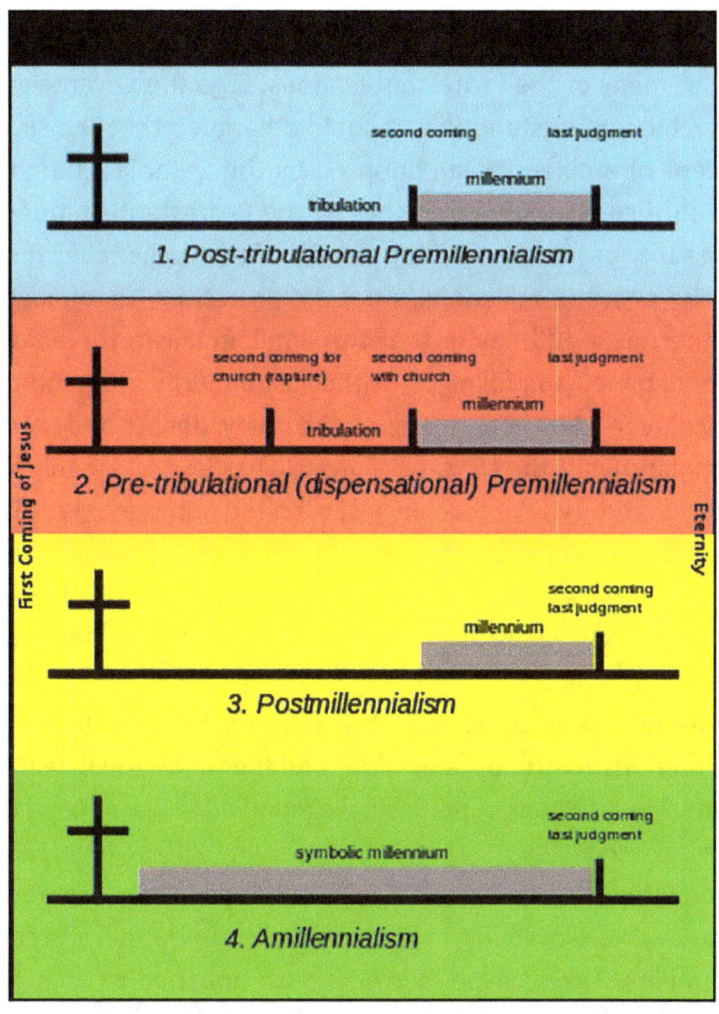

418

The point is that the hierarchy of the Catholic Church has determined and assigned a single theology to the concept of millennialism over the centuries. It is the product of theological debate and consensus by religious scholars, led by St. Augustine.[419] There is one unified position. It is not severed and scattered theology

---

[418]Id.

[419]Wikipedia, "Amillennialism."

as with many of the Protestant factions. Ergo the advantage of a hierarchy. I understand that it could be argued that the singular concept of amillennialism adopted by the Catholic Church and the more conservative branches of the Protestantism does not necessarily prove the truth or validity of that belief over the pre-trib and post trib millennialism of the Protestant denominations. But there is credibility in that the amillennialism theology has been sustained and followed by the vast majority of the Christian Church over 1,600 years, through the study, debate and teaching of scholars, while the concept of pre-trib has existed for only about 200 years through the teachings of a limited number of Protestant preachers. Even the pre-trib proponents and teachers have had at least 200 years of organized and structured debate based on scripture. Ergo, again, in either case, the advantage of the hierarchal organization.

The Jewish, Islamic, and Christian monotheistic faiths have scripture, structure, organization, and hierarchy to sustain their beliefs. Many billions of people have followed at least one of these paths as faith believers. They have not tried to do it alone. Most of the polytheistic religions also have developed their own form of literature, belief systems, formal spiritual organization, and certain hierarchies. Again, these followers have not tried to do it alone. They have aligned with a hierarchy of leaders and teachers and a body of fellow believers. In Matthew 18:15–17, Jesus tells his disciples to bring unrepented sin to the church and body of believers for resolution. The church is critical to fostering one's beliefs. It provides excellent reinforcement and a way to prevent unwitting wayward divergence from the truth of the faith. The church is the repository of the true faith, not individuals. Every believer needs to be constantly in prayer and study of the objective truths taught by the church.

Here are some real-life analogies to consider. What if the schools you attended growing up decided they would just start allowing teachers to teach whatever came to mind, with no texts, teaching plan, or coordination between the teachers? Without structure and a teaching plan, what would you expect to learn about the world and your particular areas of interest? Would you expect your physician to have attended highly structured medical schools with structured training, education, research into past medical developments, or would you give him/her the freedom to practice whatever medicine or healing art on you that came to mind? Would you allow treatment from a doctor who did not have a lengthy disciplined and structured period of focused training? Is not your spirit or soul just as important as your body, education, medical care? Your soul is just as important as your body. Wouldn't you want to dialogue with educated, experienced, and knowledgeable pastors and ministers within a more structured church environment to learn objective truths about your faith? Please remember that your physical and mental lives are but for a short finite period. Your spirit or soul exists for eternity. Please, think about it!

The point to those who claim they don't need historical religious organization or structure to formulate their belief systems are taking on an individualistic, relativistic, and self-centered stance, in my opinion. To think that one can individually figure out the truth about the Christian God, other gods or religious worldviews, atheism, polytheism, etc., on one's own without the benefit of religious hierarchy and education, structure, and organization is somewhat naïve and dangerous. Remember that we have only so many years on this earth. Some may even live to be centenarians. Or some may have their lives cut short by disease or a traumatic event such as a car accident. The point is that we don't know how long we shall live. If we don't take death as a reality and some type of eternal existence—either good or bad—as a reality, we may be sorry for eternity for not having chosen the correct spiritual path. Whatever religious worldview you adhere to or spirituality you currently believe in or don't believe in, don't try to do this on your own. If you continue to ignore organized religion and try to develop your own belief system, faith (or no faith at all), or church, you may well find yourself isolated from reality as well as from others who love you and from the true God who loves you very much. Isolationism is a slippery and dangerous slope. Think about it!

5.   Religion is not relevant to my life. Some of our youth do not see the relationship of a faith-based religion to either their physical, mental, or spiritual lives. I wonder how many of these young persons have ever really taken the time to sit down and quietly assess these relationships. I know that life, especially with all the technological advancements in accessing information, communication devices, knowledge storage innovations such as Google, extensive wealth in the hands of their parents, ability to find jobs and earn substantial income, i.e., no longer in survival mode but rather a thriving mode, sometimes distracts us from the reality of basics. However, we are no different than our ancestors but for these technological and health advancements. We just have advanced as a society. We live longer and better than our ancestors. We are still the same core human being creature as God created thousands of years ago.

The relative importance of things in our lives changes over time. When our ancestors were in survival mode, the basics of food, water and and security and protection from nature and other human beings who wanted to do them harm were most important. As our worldwide societies developed over the last 1,000 years, we began to develop solutions and over time we conquered the basics, allowing us to move on with education, scientific and philosophical research and other social and scientific breakthroughs that improved and lengthened our lives. Living into one's 50s just a few centuries ago was a remarkable feat. Today, humans have the ability to routinely live into their 80s. And within the next 50 years health and food science advancements will allow us to live into our 100s and beyond. This scientific progress is remarkable, if not miraculous, in my opinion. Unfortunately, in this rapidly advancing tech environment, God becomes less relevant or necessary with many youth, because this creates a new false sense of security in this new found self-sufficiency. That thinking is very shortsighted. First, we have God to thank for all of this. Second, this new technology does not address the health of our souls and eternal life.

And what are we doing with the gift of extra time in this physical life? Are we using it wisely to plan for the next life, which we shall experience for eternity? We focus on food, health, exercise, pastime entertainment, and many other things for our happiness in this life. Is not the eternal spiritual life hereafter at least as important as this physical life of limited duration? What are we doing as individuals and as a society to plan for eternal joy and happiness? Have we skewed the relative importance of the temporal and the eternal? Shouldn't we be spending more time focused on our soul and spirit than our physical bodies? Isn't spirituality leading to life eternal relevant and important to each of us? Think about it!

Whatever you believe or don't believe individually will not change the reality of eternal life for the rest of us. There is ample scriptural, philosophical, scientific, and factual proof that it exists. I covered all of this in earlier chapters in this book. Eternity exists. God exists. Satan exists. In one of my prior books, *Christianity on Trial: A Case for Christ*, I presented the legal evidence that proved the case for these realities. But you don't have to take my research, work, or word for it. Research it yourself. The important matter here is that you uncover and realize the truth. Do not kid yourself or let others dissuade you from the truth because, eventually, you will face it. As a Christian, I believe each of us will face Jesus to be judged first, for whether you believed in Him and secondly, for the good and bad we did during this life. How will you be judged? Is this topic of spirituality and eternity not relevant to you in the here and now? Assuming you are not atheist in your core beliefs, and further assuming your being continues on eternally because that is how and why you were created, where will you spend eternity? Think about it!

To sum up this chapter, religion should be relevant not only to this life but in preparing for the next. If we assume for argument's sake that God created you to serve Him in this life and to be with him for eternity in the next, how is that not relevant to your life? Seems to me that is the most relevant relationship you will ever have! However, God gave you free will. Only you can decide whether God is relevant to your life. Only you can determine your own future. I am suggesting in this book that religion should be a large part of your life. Our Christian God is there to help if you only ask, both in this life and into the next. He will guide you in your study and exploration of spirituality. There is an old saying within the church: "Where God guides, He provides." Let Him guide you to an eternal life of happiness and joy with Him in Heaven! He is ready. Are you? Please, think and pray about it!

CHAPTER VII

Spiritual Indifference, "Nones" and Evangelizing The "Whatever" Generation

The findings behind the reasons stated in the Pew Research piece show an alarming disconnect between our youth and spirituality. As discussed above, those who report they are unaffiliated in these surveys or in person are called "nones." The common denominator is that there is less and less concern about the life after this physical life. Our youth are taking a "whatever," nonchalant, careless attitude about their souls. They appear more concerned about the "here and now" rather than the "here and after." The consequences are dangerous and far-reaching. We missionaries and evangelists are trying our best to reach out to the indifferent and unaffiliated "nones." I presented some practical and theological responses above to counter the primary arguments raised by the unaffiliated "nones." There are new evangelical movements within the Christian church to specifically counter this trend of the unaffiliated.

The Word on Fire Institute, headed up by Catholic Bishop Robert Barron, has developed wonderful materials on understanding and evangelizing the spiritually indifferent. The Institute focuses on the spiritually indifferent. Institute leaders, Jared Zimmerer and Matt Nelson, assist the founder Bishop Robert Barron, as fellows of the institute and have developed written courses and spoken extensively on this topic.[420] I shall be referencing their excellent insights extensively throughout this chapter.

The spiritual issues described and discussed above can be categorized as "spiritual indifference." A substantial percentage of the "nones" epitomize spiritual indifference. Their numbers are rising dramatically. Over 25% of Americans report they are "nones." Today millennial "nones" amount to about 40% of the population, as noted above. Millennial Catholic "nones" amount to about 50% of that generation.[421] 33% of US cradle Catholics no longer identify as Catholics. These unaffiliated "nones" are less spiritual and religious, and less focused on God, soul, and eternal life. And for every person joining the Catholic Church, five are leaving.[422] Fewer and fewer of our youth are engaging any form of spirituality or religion for the reasons expressed above. More and more are turning to other sources to address and answer their issues of the physical universe and spirituality. Mainstream spirituality is rapidly shifting to secularism.

Summarizing the chapters above, the primary reasons "nones" are leaving the Christian Church is multifaceted, with no one predominate thing. Spiritual backsliding has occurred over time. Many "nones" don't agree with the long-held doctrines of the Catholic Church on homosexuality, contraception, and women priests. Many have had personal run-ins with the Church that has turned them off. Many don't like the way the Church has handled

---

[420]www.wordonfire.institute/courses.

[421]Barron, Bishop Robert, "Speech to Religious Education Congress," Anaheim CA, May 22, 2019; Bishop Robert Barron, "Evangelizing the Unaffiliated," Word on Fire Institute, www.wordonfire.institute/courses.

[422]Bullivant, Stephen, "Catholic Lapstation and Disaffiliation," 2019 Digital Summit, "Evangelizing the Unaffiliated," Word on Fire Institute; Bishop Barron, supra.

the recent sex-abuse scandal and crisis. And when someone leaves the Church, they find other reasons or excuses to stay away. Ex-parishioners argue that they weren't getting anything out of Mass. They note that other churches are more friendly, joyful, and more congenial and oriented toward creating a community among members. They were not feeling a sense of family or relationships in the Catholic Church. Steve Bullivant notes that the disaffected will return if they sense personal spiritual relationships with their spouse, suffering parent, and friends. These relationships lead to conversions and reversions. [423]

Bishop Barron attributes the unaffiliated movement to two primary reasons: 1) lack of belief and stopped believing in the teachings of the Church for intellectual reasons, meaning that both parents and the Church are not doing a good job explaining the faith, as noted in the chapter above; and 2) the ongoing Catholic Church sex abuse scandal, which undermines the credibility and integrity of the Church, and the Church's failure to admit sin and concupiscence of the Church like any other Christian churches but that the human side of clergy and sin is not to be conflated with the spiritual purity of the Church founded by Jesus Christ and doctrine.[424] Barron suggests these causes should be dealt with through knowledge of the faith and understanding the objections and intellectual reasoning. Evangelists need to listen and acknowledge the spiritual hurt or indifference, and remind others of the reasons for the Church.

The Church is where we reconnect with the spiritual realm and encounter Jesus through the Mass.[425] We are all called to evangelize, both clergy and lay. This is called collaborative evangelization.

---

[423]Id.

[424]Bishop Barron, supra.

[425]Id.

We are called to the Great Commission—to spread the Good News of salvation: "Therefore go and make disciples of all nations, baptizing them in the name of the Father and of the Son and of the Holy Spirit, teaching them to observe all that I commanded you" (Matthew 28:16–20).

Challenges to the faith:

Relativism. Bishop Barron notes the greatest challenges come in the form of relativism, discussed above—in parlance, "What's good for you isn't necessarily good for me. I must determine my own subjective beliefs and am fully able to believe what is best for me." This is a purely subjective stand and certainly not objective in its origin. It is a form of self-invention—"I can use my own prerogatives to invent myself." This prevalent trend has moved the younger generations from objective truth to subjective truth, left to be determined by each individual. This is a dangerous stance. There is no reliance on a higher transcendent morality. Each individual through this newfound freedom can determine what is morally right and wrong. If the trend continues, eventually, individuals will determine what is legally right and wrong, supplanting objective standards with individual standards. This becomes a serious matter in spirituality when the core beliefs and doctrines of the Church, all focused on salvation of the soul, are supplanted with individual beliefs. In other words, through relativism, the individual can supplant the proven objective truth of the teachings of God the Father and Jesus Christ the Son in the Old and New Testaments over the millennia with one's own subjective beliefs about God and eternal life. The inherent hazard and correlative risk are clear—salvation and eternal life with God. Sacred scripture and doctrine do not allow rewriting these sacred truths. In fact, both the Old and New Testaments caution against doing this: "You shall not add to the word which I am commanding you, nor take away from it, that you may keep the commandments of the Lord your God which I command you" (Deuteronomy 4:2) and "I testify to everyone who hears the words of the prophecy of this book: if anyone adds to them, God will add to him the plagues which are written in this book" (Revelation 22:18).

Atheists and agnostics use relativism to bolster their arguments against the objective truth, e.g., Jesus and Christianity. Apathetic individuals often justify their spiritual indifference with relativism. Again, the hazard is falling into one of the seven deadly sins—sloth. Again, this is a very serious spiritual matter, and the apathetic one places his/her soul in jeopardy.[426]

On a much broader philosophical level, relativism is a form of nihilism—radical subjectivism, i.e., there is no objective moral order. Nihilism is the assertion that there is no reality of faith. No proposition about morality is true—everything is arbitrary. There are no objective standards. People don't care if their positions are absurd. If there is no objective truth then relativism can become a tool of power—"I don't have to believe in your morals, and I can assert any position." Whatever one wills is the truth, therefore, one has the right to dictate what one believes. This gives one full license to implement one's own subjective belief. This leads to total and arbitrary control which in turn can lead to a true dictatorship, where the dictator does not have to answer for wrongs committed. Others can be forced to do what they don't want to do or believe.[427]

One way to deal with relativists is to lead the discussion with a subjective truth everyone can agree on—beauty. Each of us is instilled with the God given sense of creation's beauty—appealing to our basic senses of sight, sound, smell, touch, and taste. Beauty

---

[426] Id.

[427] Petrusek, Matt, "Dictatorship of Relativism," 2019 Digital Summit, Evangelizing the Unafilliated, Word on Fire Institute.

can be found both in God's creation (nature) and in our creation (art, sculpture, buildings). These are obviously products of God's beneficence creating happiness and joy in our individual lives. Another example is to argue the things that make one happy and at peace—morality and God—are both embedded in peace, happiness, joy, and contentment. The argument is then that this subjective truth must come from some true and good source—God. Goodness and truth flow from the creation of beauty. The evangelist is creating objectivity out of subjectivity to where everyone can agree. This starts the discussion.[428]

Scientism. The most common objection to the Bible is created by the conflict between science and religion. Scientism is thought or expression regarded as characteristic of scientists and excessive belief in the power of scientific knowledge and techniques, i.e., everything can be explained by one of the many scientific disciplines. There is no need or room for God. Non-believers do not have a spiritual point of reference—no church, no Bible, no spiritual fellowship, therefore, no lived witness of holiness and spirituality. Believers, on the other hand, are part of a believing community surrounded by holiness. Believers believe that religion and science are compatible.[429] Science cannot go unexplained. It is not the end all in and of itself. Rather, God created science as a tool for us to use!

Scientism is the leading philosophy of life. Basic chemistry and biology to quantum mechanics and everything in between. Science and religion are compatible. Catholics are pro-science. Science is the study of the handiwork of God. Faith and science

---

[428]Fay, Jennifer, "Happiness and the Meaning of Life," 2019 Digital Summit, Evangelizing the Unaffiliated, Word on Fire Institute; Petrusek, supra.

[429]Pagliarini, Anthony, "Misreading the Bible," 2019 Digital Summit, Evangelizing the Unaffiliated, Word on Fire Institute.

work together in the search for the truth about God. Science does not answer the fundamental questions about the meaning and purpose of life, but it does prove the existence of God.[430]

Evangelists typically use arguments based on beauty to reason goodness and truth for God, the Creator of all. They will lead with a scientific discussion about the amazing beauty and disciplines of the universe, the wonderful disciplines of science and math, sub-atomic matter and quantum mechanics, black holes, and the creation of everything through the well accepted Big Bang Theory. This is called causality. St. Thomas Aquinas argued causality as the best argument for God. [431] See my proofs and discussions above in Chapter VI. These truths are irrefutable. And they all lead back to a loving God!

Secularism. Secularism is the indifference to or rejection or exclusion of religion and religious considerations. It includes the separation of church and state. Government stays out of one's religion. They do not oppose religion, rather advocate that the state not adopt a religious preference. Secularists are nonreligious. Atheists are secularists. Secularism can include humanism, as a subset, which attaches primary importance to humans and not God and holds all things come from man and there is no need of a God. It can also include materialism, which holds that all the comforts of life can be found in the material and spirituality is not needed.

The rational evangelical argument is that the America was conceived and created by theists under the auspices of a divine power and they determined that natural law should prevail. Natural law supersedes secular law and contains the essence of morality and

---

[430]Trasancos, Stacy, "Are Faith and Science Really Enemies?" 2019 Digital Summit, Evangelizing the Unaffiliated, Word on Fire Institute.

[431]Kaczor, Chris, "Myths of the Catholic Church," 2019 Digital Summit, Evangelizing the Unaffiliated, Word on Fire Institute.

ethics and the recognition of right and wrong, good and bad. This spiritual grid, based in God, became the relational framework of this nation. Without morality and ethics superimposed on a legal structure, this society could have easily slid into moral chaos centuries ago. Natural law is a higher law creating the woven moral fabric of our nation that has not unraveled over the centuries. Legislatively created laws typically prosper one party or another in their inception. Morals and morality favor no one and create the even playing field for workable relationships. Whether the secularist likes it or not, God, in one theistic form or another, has helped this nation survive and thrive. These are the strong evangelical arguments one can use to counter secularism, humanism, and materialism.

Rationalism. The rationalists argue that reason does not support a God. They argue that one cannot reason a God and that faith is not rational. However, apologists counterargue that rational apologetics has a role to play here. 1 Peter 3:21 exhorts us to always be prepared to give a defense for hope. Apologists explain and defend faith by appealing to the rational intellect, just like the men walking on the road to Emmaus, with a "disguised" Jesus, discussing what had just happened with Jesus (Luke 24:32). Debating the facts to arrive at a logical conclusion about the power of God is the rational approach. Evangelists can find common ground with the rationalist on faith and religion, through reason. Christianity is a faith founded in historical fact, scripture, proven science, eyewitness accounts, and 2,000 years of rational debate through many councils of the Church. The truths of the Trinity, Father, Son and Holy Spirit have been proven logically and by reason.

Faith and reason are compatible. Faith is built on reason.[432] It is rational to take a leap of faith. The metaphysical can be explained by the physical. This concept has been debated over the centuries by the likes of Aquinas and Aristotle. Apologists can lead with beauty. A true Christian has a certain joy and bearing about them. They are steady in their demeanor, trusting in God through thick and thin, good and bad, valleys and mountain tops. The common thread of a Christian is hope in this world and the next. [433]

Christianity is attractive. The search for the truth of God is both exciting and exhilarating. Fellowship plus apologetics plus a good debate will lead to the spiritual truth—think the many Councils of the Catholic Church dealing with the heady issues of theology and doctrine.

Spiritual Indifference. Matt Nelson, Assistant Director, World on Fire Institute, published a book in 2018 called *Just Whatever: How to Help the Spiritually Indifferent Find Beliefs That Really Matter*. It gave a few cogent suggestions on how to assess the indifferent and how to address their lack of care about religion. I borrowed from that title in the heading of this chapter, because it so poignantly expresses the attitude of many of our youth about faith and religion—"whatever." They do not take God seriously. For the Christian faithful and clergy, it is frightening and painful to hear this lack of concern about the life hereafter. Can you imagine someone at the initial and final judgments in front of Jesus trying to explain away this attitude? What would Jesus do (WWJD)? How would He handle such as statement in his limitless compassion and mercy? My point is, why risk eternal life with a rejection or non-committal attitude toward Jesus who died for us and our sins

---

[432]Nelson, Matt, "Using Philosophy to Evangelize," 2019 Digital Summit, Word on Fire Institute; Blaise Pascal.

[433]Id.

on the cross, was resurrected from the dead and now sits at the right hand of God the Father? Jesus will be the judge. That is spiritual reality. For these reasons, all Christians are very concerned about the downward trend of committed believers who actually care and are engaged with their Christian faith. What will happen to the spiritually indifferent? No one knows for certain, but scripture certainly gives us strong clues.

To these points, Nelson names and addresses the different types and levels of indifference and their causes:

Closed Religious Indifference (CRI). Rejects all religions as untrue. Non-theists reject a supernatural and spiritual God and a relationship with Him. All religions are meaningless. They are caught up in secularism and materialism instead. Their philosophy is relativism, which is the primary atheist worldview. No God is greater than man. Man rises to the level of a God and is self-sufficient. Man becomes God. Men become masters of their own world and destiny. Modern man places himself on the top of the food chain. Relativism is the primary philosophy of CRI cohort.[434]

Scientism also has a role to play here as CRIs feel they can explain much of the universe through science. No need for a creationist God. We are at the top of the food chain.

Materialism holds that everything comes from the material world and can be explained in reality. No need for spirituality.

Much of this CRI thinking is driven by the technological developments and advancements over the last 60 years. Smart tech can now "answer" most of man's questions about life and existence. Doctrinal authority is off-putting for the CRIs. It becomes "preachy" and unnecessary to them. Interestingly, many CRI's maintain some level of spiritual belief because they recognize that smart tech

---

[434] Nelson, Matt, "The Problem of Religious Indifference, Reaching the Indifferent," Word on Fire Institute.

can't answer all the questions especially those related to the meaning and purpose of life or the creation of the universe with the Big Bang, Man being created in the image of God, how the mind, emotions, conscience and the innate drive toward a higher supernatural power work. Many unanswered questions! And relativism, secularism, and materialism (physical reality) all fail to recognize the clear arguments for and proof of the existence of God, as discussed above in chapter VI.

Atheists hold to the philosophy that all that exists is physical reality. Relativism holds that we are free to do whatever we wish irrespective of the consequences. The philosophical sum for CRIs is that there is no God. Life is purposeless and evolution meaningless. We are all headed to oblivion. And because there is no God, we are doomed without value or purpose and there is no hope of life after death.[435]

How do we confront CRIs? With the truth. With a moral argument pointing to the solid evidence and proof of God's existence. The argument centers on moral truth. Everyone can agree that certain actions are objectively wrong. Immanuel Kant is quoted as saying, "Moral reality is within me." He tried to merge morality and free will. Moral law binds all people and is objective in application. Physical laws describe what is. Moral laws describe what ought to be and moral experience controls our speech and thoughts. Moral laws lead us to God.[436] The moral argument for God can be structured as follows: 1) if objective moral truths exist, then God exists, 2) objective truths exist, therefore 3) God exists. Where does this absolute and objective moral standard come from? God! We imperfect and sinful humans need an objective perfect moral

---

[435]Nelson, Matt, "Why We Should Believe in a Spiritual Reality, Reaching the Indifferent," Word on Fire Institute.

[436]Nelson, Matt, "Why You Can't be Good without God, Reaching the Indifferent," Word ono Fire Insititute.

standard of goodness. The standard of laws/statutes created by man often do not reach to levels of morality. We need to reach higher. Remember we are made in the image of God. Shouldn't we also be expected to conduct ourselves the best we can, according to His character? Shouldn't we strive to be as morally perfect as He is? I say we should! However, CRIs contend moral relativism holds that humans determine their own morality standard or that of the majority. What happens when the individual or society making the laws stray from the perfect objective standards of God? That world begins to implode in chaos. God knows best! And God is the only logical source for moral truth!

We can evangelize the CRIs with this moral argument. However, please note that this philosophical argument is in addition to the hard historic, scientific, and scriptural evidentiary proof of the existence of God above. The evangelist has many tools at hand.

Open Religious Indifferent (ORI). Anything goes in religion. ORIs lower Jesus to the level of other gods. There is nothing special about Jesus. He is a mere prophet. He is not divine. He is not a God any more important than any other. All religions are equally good and true. ORIs claim an open mindedness to all religions even though they are contradictory in their doctrines. This philosophy is a theistic philosophy subject to relativism. Theology is determined by people less concerned about doctrine than convenience.[437]

ORI avoids the search for truth. What is one true faith? To the ORI it makes no difference. To those truly seeking the truth they will be inclined to match up one religion with the other. I did this in my second book, *Christianity on Trial: A Case for Christ*, to prove the divinity of Christ and the truth of the Christian faith. I shall do it again here for our readers' convenience. Jesus Christ

---

[437] Nelson, Matt, "The Problem of Religious Indifference, Reaching the Indifferent," Word on Fire Institute.

and Christianity win hands down, for the following reasons: 1) Jesus is prophesized in many the Old Testament—forward allusion, 2) Jesus miraculously conceived by the Holy Spirit; 3) Jesus performed many recorded miracles and innumerable unrecorded miracles during his three-year ministry on earth; 4) Jesus was crucified for our sins and the salvation of mankind, died (confirmed by a 1980s JAMA article on the death of Christ) was buried, was resurrected and rose from the dead; 5) Jesus appeared in the flesh to His disciples and many of his followers, 6) Jesus miraculously appeared in a locked room, in the flesh, to St. Thomas who placed his hand into Jesus' side, 7) Jesus physically ate with his disciples and followers, 8) Jesus claimed to be God and proved he was a divine God by all the above, 9) Jesus physically ascended into heaven in the presence of his disciples who were greeted by two angels. He is not just a legend or a historical figure. Jesus is the real and divine God. Jesus was reported to be a true historical figure by eyewitnesses and scholars—both believers and nonbelievers. St Luke, the physician, as an excellent historian and reported extensively and accurately on the factual history of Jesus, in his Gospel.

No other historical religious figure can claim the self-sacrifice of a person such as Jesus for the salvation of humanity and the opportunity for eternal life with God the Father and God the Son. No other figure gave their life in total sacrifice for another. No other religious figure has ever claimed they were God. No other figure worked any legitimate proven miracles while on earth. No other figure ever showed the love, compassion, and mercy for common man to help them in this life and to open the doors of heaven to receive them after death for eternal life with God. And no other figure was ever resurrected from the dead!

Denominational Indifference (DI). DI is the aversion toward doctrine or taking denominational differences seriously. DI's waive the contradictions between Catholics and Protestants by rejecting dogma, as long we worship the same God.[438]

Protestants claim back to the time of Luther—1,500 AD. Protestants offer a personal relationship with Christ and each other by appealing to the emotional and personal side. There are over 40,000 different Protestant denominations. Many denominations believe in Sola Fida—salvation by faith alone. They look to scripture as the entire authority of the church—Sola Scriptura. Protestants are centered on the word—scripture.

Catholics are centered in Jesus through the sacrament of the Eucharist. Catholics are a sacramental Church. They look to both scripture and tradition. 2,000 years of tradition help interpret the meaning of scriptural passages. Catholics argue that the Catholic Church claims a heritage all the way back to its founder, Jesus. Peter was the first of 267 popes of the church forming the magisterium. Catholics offer 1) unity in truth through doctrine, 2) unity in Christ through the sacraments, and 3) unity in the Church through the saints.[439]

These are the basic differences. The question is which one is closer to the truth established by Christ Himself. Catholics believe Jesus is interested in orthodoxy to preserve the true doctrine. No room for false teaching. Apostolic teachings are primary, because they are closest in time to Jesus. They are found in the New Testament Gospels, books, and letters. These scriptural sources created the fundamental Christian doctrines that are still used today, 2,000 years later. Doctrine is a function of both the head and heart. Therefore, authors must both know God and love God. St. Paul reminds to "watch life and doctrine carefully" (1 Tim 4:16).

---

[438]Nelson, Matt, "The Problem with Religious Indifference, and Who is Jesus?" Reaching the Indifferent, Word on Fire Istitute

[439]Nelson, Matt, "Orthodoxy Matters, Reaching the Indifferent," Word on Fire Institute.

The primary doctrines of the Catholic Church are: 1) incarnation, 2) divinity of Christ, 3) Holy Trinity, 3) Bible as the inspired word of God, and 4) personal relationship with God.[440]

The primary conflict between Protestants and Catholics is the Catholic Magisterium—subservience and obedience to the Pope as the leader of the church. Secondly, Protestants do not accept the traditions of the Catholic Church (Catechism). However, Catholics believe they find their spiritual authority from 1) sacred scripture, 2) sacred tradition (doctrine) and 3) Magisterium. The Magisterium is deemed to be former and protector of the faith. The secondary conflict is authority of sacred tradition as mentioned above. Catholics believe they have the fullness of the faith.

The Catholic evangelist can address the doctrinal schism by 1) engaging in intellectual dialogue and arguments and 2) teaching children to think clearly.

---

[440]Id.

CHAPTER VIII

The Challenge of Making The Right Decision

I wrote this book to challenge the younger Gen Y and Gen Z era to re-examine their priorities in life. We all have experienced how exciting it is to live in these times. Everything moves so quickly. Everything anyone could possibly want to enjoy in this life is at hand—every conceivable product can be purchased off eBay, Amazon, Walmart, or at Costco! Nothing is left to the imagination except for new inventions, technologies, and medicines, all which will make our lives even better. We are comfortable in this Western civilization. Certainly, there are billions living in third-world countries who have barely enough to survive. Many still starve to death today while we live in abundance. We are indeed blessed beyond belief!

I believe we need to voluntarily share our material and spiritual wealth to help bring these forlorn and lost peoples into the twenty-first century. I understand this is a huge undertaking, but I believe we who have been so richly blessed should reach out in "love of neighbor" to lend a hand. Not in a politically socialist-mandated manner but rather in a loving voluntary cheerful Christian manner. To accomplish this great feat, I believe we need to leave any self-centeredness and egos behind. God loves a cheerful giver. After all He created us in love to love Him back as well as one another. Life is all about love! It is also about knowing Him, and sharing Him with others, all in love. Please consider how you might increase your "love offerings" back to God and others. Once you get into the habit of tithing back and giving to neighbor, your life will never be the same. This will change you. Can you begin to forgive others who have hurt you? That is also part of God's great love story. I am about to make a very bold proclamation here—life is not about you. It is not about neighbor. It is not about God. Instead it is about God, your neighbor, and you all living in a very intimate and loving relationship with one another. It is about *love*! This is the sum total of scriptural teaching in the Jewish Old Testament and the Christian New Testament.

Even in these times, many people have missed the message from God—His intent for each of us and the reason for creating each of us. Those performing the corporal and spiritual works of mercy get it. Those who devote their lives in service of others in need get it. Those who care for the elderly, sick, and infirm get it. Teachers, doctors, social workers, and first responder police and firemen and mothers get it. We seem to be losing some of the balance in loving God first, neighbor second, and ourselves third. This is a paraphrase of the Great Commandment given to us by Jesus, noted above in earlier chapters (Matthew 22:35–40 and Mark 12:28–34). God gave us the same message back in the Old Testament. Deuteronomy 6:4–5 and Leviticus 19:18. John, the evangelist, also reminds us what Jesus tells us to love one another as He has loved us (John 13:34). Again, the sum of God's intent and purpose for each of in both the Old and New Testaments of the Bible can be netted down to one word—*love*!

We know that Jesus came from Heaven, became man, suffered and died an ignominious death on the cross at the hands of the Jews and Romans, all for the forgiveness of man's sins and for the salvation of humankind. We just need to accept the grace of His gift of forgiveness and salvation by believing in Jesus, repenting of our sins evidenced by Baptism, and thereafter confessing our sins and leading holy lives. To lead a holy life in love of God and neighbor is to obey God's original Ten Commandments and Jesus' Great Commandment. It is that simple. Eternal life with your creator, savior, and guardian (Father, Son and Holy Spirit) can be that simple. It is all a matter of attitude, gratitude, and love!

To obtain this grace of the gift of forgiveness of sin through the redemptive work of Jesus and salvation into eternal life with God requires us to change our attitude about God and neighbor. We need to leave sins behind and begin to acquire the graces and blessings of God. We need to be grateful for these gifts. And we need to share them with others. This is to know God and to share Him with others. This is the mantra and core belief of YWAM (Youth with a Mission) the largest non-denominational missionary movement in the world. These volunteers (in excess of 30,000) have largely left worldly possessions and belongings behind, much as Jesus' disciples and followers. They administer to the needs of millions of people annually, mostly in third-world nations following the Great Commission. They live Jesus' Great Commandment. This is not say, however, that everyone must follow this meritorious example literally, but we all must at least follow the spiritual basis— love of God and neighbor. Ask yourself what you can do for your family, next-door neighbor, strangers you meet along the way with obvious physical, mental and financial challenges. What can you do to make a difference in their lives? And how much time could you devote daily in prayer to give glory, praise, and thanksgiving back to your God and Creator. Catch my point? It's all about love!

Are you ready to leave some the physical and financial baggage of this world behind and begin to build up treasure in heaven?

Do not store up for yourselves treasures on earth, where moth and rust destroy, and where thieves break in and steal. But store up for yourselves treasures in heaven, where neither moth nor rust destroys, and where thieves do not break in or steal; for where your treasure is, there your heart will be also (Matthew 6:19-21; NASB).

This is an important step in rebalancing our temporal and spiritual lives toward what is important and what is not. Please consider the observations and suggestions in this book as a start of a lifelong process. It is important for you and your family. The consequences are permanent and forever. Please choose wisely.

See you on the other side!

ABOUT THE AUTHOR

Dave grew up in Southern California, attended the University of California, Riverside, and graduated in 1966 with an AB in Geology/Geophysics. He attended the University of San Diego School of Law, graduated in 1969 with a JD, and was admitted to the CA bar in 1970.

In 1969, Dave met and married his law school sweetheart, Trudy. She was in the nurse training program at the University of San Diego School of Nursing.

In 1970 during the Vietnam War, he was drafted and served in the USAF Judge Advocate Corps (JAGC). Beginning in 1972, Dave served at McChord Air Force Base in WA as an area defense counsel, handling criminal cases. He was admitted to the Washington bar. In 1975, Dave was assigned to the US Air Force's JAG headquarters office in in Washington, DC, as an appellate defense counsel. Evenings, he attended Georgetown University Law Center, where he was awarded an LLM degree in International Law in 1978. That same year, Dave left active duty, moved back to WA State, and transferred into the Air Force JAG Reserves at McChord AFB. He was later promoted to the rank of Colonel and reassigned to Travis AFB in CA, where he eventually retired in 1997. Starting in 1978, Dave served as an Assistant Attorney General for WA State representing the Department of Natural Resources for four years.

In 1982, Dave started his own law practice in Olympia, WA, where he practiced general law for 23 years until 2005.

Dave's wife, Trudy, practiced as an RN in a number of ERs across the country beginning in 1969. She retired from nursing in 2005. In 2005, Dave and Trudy, had an opportunity to move to Kona, Hawaii, to purchase Heavenly Hawaiian Farms, a 38.5 acre start-up Kona coffee farm, where they have been farming, giving tours, and selling coffee around the world ever since. In 2014, Dave and Trudy started up a roasting operation just north of Dallas, TX, with two wonderful Christian partners, Pacific Tradewinds Coffee Co, LLC, dba, TexaKona. These are Christian businesses that have been dedicated to the service of God and neighbor.

In 2008, Dave and Trudy had the privilege of participating in a YWAM DTS (Youth with a Mission, Discipleship Training Program) where they grew in their knowledge about God and how to share Him with others. Later, they served on outreach in the Cook Islands and Fiji, sharing the love and word of God. Dave served on the board of trustees of the University of the Nations, Kona, for six years and also served as general counsel for the University. Dave and Trudy attend St Michael's Catholic Church in Kailua-Kona, where they both serve various ministries. They have also been involved in many Bible study programs over the years in Washington and Hawaii.

www.ingramcontent.com/pod-product-compliance
Lightning Source LLC
LaVergne TN
LVHW021957060526
838201LV00048B/1606